Equality and Diversity in Social Work Practice

Equality and Diversity in Social Work Practice

Edited by

CHRIS GAINE

Series Editors: Jonathan Parker and Greta Bradley

LearningMatters

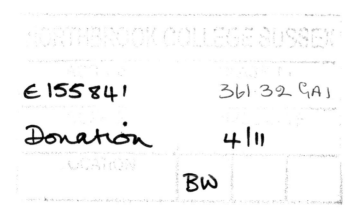
First published in 2010 by Learning Matters Ltd

© 2010 Gill Constable (Chapter 4); Chris Gaine, Introduction (Chapters 1, 3, 9 and 10); David Gaylard (Chapter 1); Colin Goble (Chapter 5); Gianna Knowles (Chapter 7); Vini Lander (Chapter 8); Janet McCray (Chapter 6); Barbara Thompson (Chapter 2)

British Library Cataloguing in Publication Data
A CIP record for this book is available from the British Library

ISBN 978 1 84445 593 5

This book is also available in the following ebook formats:
Adobe ebook ISBN: 978 184445 757 1
EPUB ebook ISBN: 978 184445 756 4
Kindle ISBN: 978 0857 2501 93

The right of Gill Constable, Chris Gaine, David Gaylard, Colin Goble, Gianna Knowles, Vini Lander, Janet McCray and Barbara Thompson to be identified as the Authors of this Work has been asserted by them in accordance with the Copyright, Designs and Patents Act 1988.

Text and cover design by Code 5 Design Associates Ltd
Project Management by Deer Park Productions, Tavistock
Typeset by Pantek Arts Ltd, Maidstone, Kent
Printed and bound in Great Britain by Bell & Bain Ltd, Glasgow

Learning Matters Ltd
33 Southernhay East
Exeter EX1 1NX
Tel: 01392 215560
E-mail: info@learningmatters.co.uk
www.learningmatters.co.uk

Contents

Introduction vii

1 **Equality, difference and diversity** 1
Chris Gaine and David Gaylard

2 **Gender** 17
Barbara Thompson

3 **Sexual orientation** 29
Chris Gaine

4 **Older people** 42
Gill Constable

5 **Celebrating disability** 55
Colin Goble

6 **Learning disabilities** 66
Janet McCray

7 **Class** 75
Gianna Knowles

8 **Race and ethnicity** 88
Vini Lander

9 **Faith and religion** 102
Chris Gaine

Conclusion 116
Chris Gaine

Glossary 123

References 127

Index 141

Introduction

This book is written for student social workers who are beginning to develop their skills and understanding of the requirements for practice. While it is primarily aimed at students in their first year or level of study, it will be useful for subsequent years depending on how your programme is designed, what you are studying and especially as you move into practice learning. The book will also appeal to people considering a career in social work or social care but not yet studying for a social work degree. It will assist students undertaking a range of social and health care courses in further education. Nurses, occupational therapists and other health and social care professionals will be able to gain an insight into the new requirements demanded of social workers. Experienced and qualified social workers, especially those contributing to practice learning, will also be able to use this book for consultation, teaching and revision and to gain an insight into the expectations raised by the qualifying degree in social work.

Requirements for social work education

Social work education has undergone a major transformation to ensure that qualified social workers are educated to honours degree level and develop knowledge, skills and values which are common and shared. A vision for social work operating in complex human situations has been adopted. This is reflected in the following definition from the International Association of Schools of Social Work and International Federation of Social Workers (2001).

> The social work profession promotes social change, problem solving in human relationships and the empowerment and liberation of people to enhance well-being. Utilising theories of human behaviour and social systems, social work intervenes at the points where people interact with their environments. Principles of human rights and social justice are fundamental to social work.

While there is a great deal packed into this short and pithy definition it encapsulates the notion that social work concerns individual people and wider society. Social workers practise with people who are vulnerable, who are struggling in some way to participate fully in society. Social workers walk that tightrope between the marginalised individual and the social and political environment that may have contributed to their marginalisation, and they need to be highly skilled and knowledgeable to work effectively in this context.

In order to improve the quality of both these aspects of professional social work, it is crucial that you, as a student social worker, develop a rigorous grounding in and understanding of theories and models for social work. Such knowledge helps social workers to know what to do, when to do it and how to do it, while recognising that social work is a complex activity with no absolute 'rights' and 'wrongs' of practice for each situation.

The book aims to meet the learning needs outlined in the Department of Health's prescribed curriculum for competence in assessment, planning, intervention and review, incorporating the necessary knowledge, skills and development of values. It will also meet subject skills identified in the Quality Assurance Agency academic benchmark criteria for social work. This approach will draw on and rely on you to acquire high-quality communication skills, skills in working with others, and reflective skills in personal and professional development. In essence, the book will concentrate on models that are current in practice and transferable across settings. An action-oriented approach helps to facilitate evaluation and review of your practice. Case studies will be used throughout to enhance this process and to illustrate key points.

Book structure

Research indicates that social workers vary considerably in the extent to which they make and test hypotheses in practice (Sheppard, et al., 2001). A shift towards understanding 'knowledge as process' as opposed to 'knowledge as product' is suggested as one way to integrate theory and practice. These changes to social work education and the implementation of new degree courses mean that there is a need for new, practical learning support material to help you achieve the qualification. This book is designed to help you gain knowledge concerning assessment, planning, intervention and review, to reflect on that knowledge and to apply it in practice. The emphasis in this book concerns you achieving the requirements of the curriculum and developing knowledge that will assist you in meeting the Occupational Standards for social work.

The book has ten chapters. The opening and concluding chapters offer ways of integrating the insights of individual chapters and seeing parallels and similarities while the rest deal with a specific aspect of diversity or kind of inequality (and the book dwells a good deal on these alternative ways of seeing). In fact the title of this book was subject to some debate. We nearly called it *Dealing with inequality and injustice in social work practice*, but in the end we didn't because, although it would have been an accurate title, we wanted a more positive tone. While we discuss much in the way of negative experiences and destructive social processes we also believe it is possible to make a difference, and for social workers to make a difference.

This book aims to give an introduction to issues that we know raise difficulties in social work practice and in social work training. In principle the concerns of the book seem simple: people should be treated with justice, and some might wonder how that can be problematic to a profession committed to supporting and enabling people to overcome obstacles in their lives and live to their full potential. The answer is twofold. First, the world we live in is beset with injustices of various kinds and they are embedded in the way systems operate and individuals think, so they are difficult to challenge and often even more difficult to change. Second, we ourselves are embedded in many ways of thinking connected to injustice; to different extents we grow up with them and take some for granted, so a personal engagement with the issues in this book can at times be uncomfortable, even threatening.

It can also be liberating. The prejudicial attitudes we all have to some degree towards one group or another limit us from seeing one another's humanity, and indeed ration and limit our own. We hope you will recognise distortions in your own perceptions as you go through the book and work through them, and we hope you will actively engage both your emotional and your intellectual self. It's not likely you'll significantly increase your insight into these matters unless you do both; at times you need empathy to put yourself in another's place but you also need analytical thought to critique ways of seeing the world.

As you will see in chapter after chapter, the social meaning of gender, sexual orientation, age, disability, class, race and religion are not to be taken for granted and are not static. Within the lifetime of anyone reading this book some aspects of this diversity were illegal (gay sex under 21 was only legalised 15 years ago) while job discrimination against disabled people was perfectly legal until around the same time. You only have to be a little older to have seen successive battles to ensure equal pay for equivalent work, irrespective of gender. Laws can change behaviour and there is some evidence that resistant attitudes will be modified as a result, but it's never quick, so you live and work in a set of complex and unpredictable currents. You can't be sure when a service user in her 80s will tell you she's a lesbian, or a Chinese client will exhibit great antipathy to a learning disabled relative, or a black colleague will refer to council tenants as chavs, or you yourself will find yourself looking at one of your own preconceptions right in the eye.

Your professional standards are uncompromising about this. You have to work at providing an equitable service to clients while dealing with or fending off challenges related to diversity. But professional standards say where you have to get to; they are standards against which you will be judged. We hope that reading and reflecting on the information, arguments and activities in the book will help with the journey.

Learning features

The book is interactive. You are encouraged to work through the book as an active participant, taking responsibility for your learning, in order to increase your knowledge, understanding and ability to apply this learning to practice. You will be expected to reflect creatively on how immediate learning needs can be met in the areas of assessment, planning, intervention and review and how your professional learning can be developed in your future career.

Case studies throughout the book will help you to examine theories and models for social work practice. We have devised activities that require you to reflect on experiences, situations and events and help you to review and summarise learning undertaken. In this way your knowledge will become deeply embedded as part of your development. When you come to practise learning in an agency the work and reflection undertaken here will help you to improve and hone your skills and knowledge. Suggestions for further reading will be made at the end of each chapter and at the end is a glossary to help clarify many of the contested terms in this field.

Professional development and reflective practice

Great emphasis is placed on developing skills of reflection about, in and on practice. This has developed over many years in social work. It is important also that you reflect prior to practice, if indeed this is your goal. This book will assist you in developing a questioning approach that looks in a critical way at your thoughts, experiences and practice and seeks to heighten your skills in refining your practice as a result of these deliberations. Reflection is central to good social work practice, but only if action results from that reflection.

Reflecting about, in and on your practice is not only important during your education to become a social worker; it is considered key to continued professional development. As we move to a profession that acknowledges lifelong learning as a way of keeping up to date, ensuring that research informs practice and in honing skills and values for practice, it is important to begin the process at the outset of your development.

Chapter 1

Equality, difference and diversity

Chris Gaine and David Gaylard

A C H I E V I N G   A   S O C I A L   W O R K   D E G R E E

This chapter will help you meet the following National Occupational Standards.

Key Role 1: Prepare for, and work with individuals, families, carers, groups and communities to assess their needs and circumstances.

- Prepare for social work contact and involvement.
- Work with individuals, families, carers, groups and communities to help them make informed decisions.

Key Role 2: Plan, carry out, review and evaluate social work practice, with individuals, families, carers, groups, communities and other professionals.

- Interact with individuals, families, carers, groups and communities to achieve change and development and to improve life opportunities.

Key Role 3: Support individuals to represent their needs, views and circumstances.

- Advocate with, and on behalf of, individuals, families, carers, groups and communities.

Key Role 6: Demonstrate professional competence in social work practice.

- Research, analyse, evaluate and use current knowledge of best social work practice.

It will also introduce you to the following academic standards as set out in the social work subject benchmark statement.

5.1.1 Social work services, service users and carers.

- Explanations of the links between definitional processes contributing to social differences (for example, social class, gender, ethnic differences, age, sexuality and religious belief) to the problems of inequality and differential need faced by service users.
- The nature of social work services in a diverse society (with particular reference to concepts such as prejudice, interpersonal, institutional and structural discrimination, empowerment and anti-discriminatory practices).

5.1.3 Values and ethics.

- The moral concepts of rights, responsibility, freedom, authority and power inherent in the practice of social workers as moral and statutory agents.

5.5.3 Analysis and synthesis.

- Assess the merits of contrasting theories, explanations, research, policies and procedures.
- Critically analyse and take account of the impact of inequality and discrimination in work with people in particular contexts and problem situations.

Introduction

Human diversity is a concept with lots of layers. It can just refer to differences, like height, hair colour, whether you have freckles or the kind of food you like, but the kind of diversity that matters to social workers is diversity with social significance, diversity that makes real differences to people's lives. We don't know much about whether or not being six feet tall affects someone's chances of getting a job, but we do know that their gender, age and social class do. In the UK and much of Europe there are six aspects of diversity that are felt to have sufficient social significance to need laws about them: gender, sexual orientation, religion, race and ethnicity, age and disability (and social class may soon join them). The Equality and Human Rights Commission, whose job it is to promote fair treatment, refers to these as seven protected groups. In other words, there is evidence of and official concern about these aspects of diversity potentially leading to injustice and inequality.

The view of the law, therefore, and the profession of social work, is that it is morally and legally right, socially desirable and economically sensible to challenge and combat discrimination, promote equal opportunity and value difference. It is also worth asserting the positive value of diversity; it can be viewed as a good thing that should be celebrated, something that enriches our lives, introducing us to new ideas or approaches. In this context we prefer the word 'acceptance' to 'tolerance'. There is something about tolerance that implies 'putting up with', so you might tolerate noisy neighbours but is the same word appropriate for your approach to disabled neighbours?

Feelings and attitudes

These issues provoke strong feelings, and indeed a discussion we have sometimes had with students is which of the social inequalities would start the most heated argument in a pub. It's not that we like arguing in pubs, but it's a fair test of how controversial a topic is, and for social workers it's an index of how much they may be countering others' deep-seated attitudes, or indeed their own. Our feeling is that while all the inequalities covered in this book can generate strong opinions when discussed, disability might evoke pity; learning difficulties some embarrassment; gender differences some attempts at humour; age perhaps some wry impatience and indulgence; social class can induce feelings of superiority (or inferiority); religion a degree of intolerance; race scores highly in the argument league as regards anger, while sexual orientation will often be the subject of distaste or even disgust.

ACTIVITY **1.1**

The previous paragraph is summarised in this table, which you might want to modify or add to.

	Most common emotional response evoked in discussions	Other reactions?
Disability		
Learning difficulties		
Gender		
Age		
Social class		
Religion		
Race and ethnicity		
Sexual orientation		

Comment

Whatever you have written in response to this table, it will be obvious that one cannot engage with social inequalities without encountering your own and others' emotions. In principle our professional rules are clear; in practice there are minefields to cross.

Two key concepts

While individual chapters contain some specific definitions and there is also a glossary, we think there are two key concepts that need clarifying early in this book. The first is *prejudice*, which is best defined as a learned attitude towards a group of people (and hence individuals from that group) that is based upon a stereotype and founded more on emotion than rationality and is therefore relatively resistant to change. Such attitudes are used to pre-judge people. Strictly speaking prejudice can be positive: because of the stereotype you hold about them (a simplified and inflexible idea of what most people in the group are like) you might be positively prejudiced towards other mature students, supporters of your own football team or people who wear anti-war badges. But it's most commonly meant in the negative sense – prejudice against women drivers, white van men, refugees, Conservatives, Jehovah's Witnesses, lecturers who ask you to 'share', obese people, smokers, 4 × 4 drivers and so on (the list of potential prejudices could go on for several pages). Everyone has prejudices, including the authors of this book; no one is immune. Some Jews have prejudices towards non-Jews, some gay men have prejudices about straight men, some disabled people don't like Asians, and some blind people have prejudices about sighted people.

Social identity theory (sometimes referred to as self-categorisation theory) sheds some light on this general tendency we all share as human beings. The main tenets of the theory are as follows.

- *Categorisation* A need to put others (and ourselves) into categories. Labelling someone a Muslim, a chav or a football supporter is a way of saying other things about them. This produces an accentuation effect, an apparent conceptual clarity by emphasising differences or similarities between different groups or categories.

- *Identification* A need to associate with certain groups (in-groups) which serve to bolster our self-esteem.

- *Stereotypes* The categorisation process produces stereotypical perceptions that all members of a social group share some characteristic which distinguishes them from other social groups. These are based upon incorrect subjective beliefs or generalisations.

- *Comparison* Comparing groups with other groups, seeing favourable bias toward the group we belong to.

- *Psychological distinctiveness* We desire our identity to be both distinct and positively compared with other groups.

(Tajfel and Turner, 1979)

Some prejudices might be thought of as relatively harmless, but a problem for us as professionals arises when they are unexamined, or inflexible, or stubbornly clung to.

The second key concept is related but not the same: *discrimination*. Again there is a strict definition which simply means choosing (I might discriminate between France and Italy in choosing a holiday) but as with prejudice our interest here is with discriminating against, and particularly discrimination on irrelevant or unjust criteria, as discussed in the next section. Discrimination is an action, whereas prejudice is an attitude: one is in your mind; the other is in what you do.

It's possible to be prejudiced without discriminating (an estate agent may not like Pakistanis but nevertheless sell their houses) and it's possible to discriminate without being prejudiced (by just obeying orders) but they are often linked, and the link is most dangerous and damaging when power is involved. Officials of all kinds, including social workers, have the power to act upon their prejudices, and this is where discrimination translates difference into disadvantage. For people in a minority of some kind, there is a risk of being positioned and limited by the prejudice and related discrimination of those in the majority or those with more power. This is illustrated in Figure 1.1.

When is difference relevant?

A key thing to bear in mind about the connection between diversity, injustice and inequality is the issue of relevance. We have to make careful judgements (and sometimes we'll get it wrong) about when some feature of a person's identity is relevant or not in a particular context. For instance, in employing someone as a community transport driver is it relevant that one applicant is black, Jewish, a lesbian, sixty years old and has dyslexia? Most people would probably say that a person's skin colour as such has nothing to do with their driving ability; neither has who they go to bed with, nor whether they're male or female, nor what their religious beliefs may be. However, one could (and people do) think up arguments saying they are relevant, for instance:

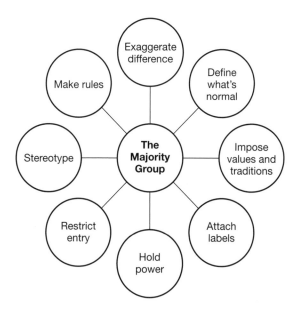

Figure 1.1 Strategies by which majority groups keep control and hold power

Adapted from Clements and Spinks (2008)

- *Race* 'Some older people using community transport may be prejudiced against black people, so they'd lose out if they didn't use the bus (and it's their country after all, they fought in the war, etc., etc.).'

- *Sexual orientation* 'Vulnerable people using community transport might be preyed upon by homosexuals.'

- *Religion* 'Some people might need to be picked up or dropped off at churches or church facilities; a Jew wouldn't like to go into a church.'

- *Gender* 'Women don't drive big vehicles as well as men.'

- *Age* 'Maybe an older driver wouldn't be strong enough to help someone infirm on and off the bus.'

- *Disability* 'A dyslexic driver might deliver someone to the wrong address.'

You will have your own reactions to those arguments, and indeed it's worth considering and rehearsing them since, as a social worker, you will often have to think clearly and logically (and engage creatively and constructively with others) about these issues. What may strike you is that some people will regard the points above as absurd and outrageous, while others will not. Some individuals you know, and some service users, probably think gay people are constantly wanting to seduce anyone of the same sex; others will have patronising attitudes about women drivers; others will think a person's right not to be upset by contact with black people should take precedence over a black person's right to a job.

The law is very clear that all the suggested arguments above are misconceived and inappropriate: the right to be employed irrespective of various aspects of one's identity trumps them all. If the driver needs to be physically strong then that requirement has to be in the job description, and there are strong, fit people of 60 and weak ones of 25. If a disability might affect someone's capacity to do the job it's the employer's legal duty to provide support and make 'reasonable adjustments'. If bus users don't like black people it's not the responsibility of the provider to accommodate their prejudices.

ACTIVITY *1.2*

To think about this more, try substituting other occupations (like nurse, home support worker, airline pilot or police officer) and substituting other variants of six aspects of diversity (Muslim instead of Jewish, blind instead of dyslexic, age 20 rather than 60).

Comment

Generally the process of substituting other occupations and other aspects of diversity highlights taken-for-granted assumptions. This can be useful for your own development but is also a useful tool for you in the inevitable discussions you will have with colleagues and clients. The Quality Assurance Agency expects social workers to *understand the impact of injustice, social inequalities and oppressive social relations, and challenge constructively individual, institutional and structural discrimination* (QAA, 2008, Section 4.6).

Shifting perspectives about relevance

The issue of relevance is not simple. Most of us have assumptions about aspects of diversity we haven't had much to do with or just haven't thought through, and anyway, general attitudes shift and change over time. Only 20 years ago the Conservative government at the time passed a law containing something fairly hostile to gay people, arguing that sexual orientation was relevant to their employment, especially as teachers; the law has since been repealed and the Conservative leader apologised in 2009 that it became law in the first place. The Local Government Act 1988, Section 28: *a local authority shall not intentionally promote homosexuality or publish material with the intention of promoting homosexuality* or *promote the teaching in any maintained school of the acceptability of homosexuality as a pretended family relationship*. Women used to be able to retire earlier than men (even though for decades they had on average outlived them); this was rooted in a wider set of beliefs that the workplace wasn't really for them anyway. Until 1968 it was perfectly legal to refuse to let a flat to someone on racial or ethnic grounds; until 1976 it remained legal to refuse if you had to share a bathroom with a black tenant. In these three examples, social attitudes have largely moved on, but not everyone has moved on with them and you are likely to find yourself in the front line of engaging with social attitudes about diversity because of the personal work social workers do with people. If one goes further back the contrasts are more dramatic: until 1967 men were sent to prison if caught in homosexual acts; most women were not considered capable of voting until 1928; separate schools for children with all kinds of disabilities were widespread until the 1970s. The monarch is still not allowed to marry a Catholic.

Naturally this book dwells on the consequences for clients of unequal treatment and inadequate recognition of diversity, but in practice this is indivisible from how we treat colleagues. A study of the Metropolitan Police in the 1980s quoted an inspector as saying *I freely admit I hate, loathe and despise black people. I don't let it affect my job though.* This is not a tenable position; disrespect, suspicion, distaste, mockery, condescension, fear or outright dislike of colleagues because they belong to one or more of the groups dealt with in this book will inevitably have an impact upon clients. In a work climate featuring any of these negative attitudes it's not likely anyone will work to their best ability, and indeed talented staff who become alienated, with their potential to improve clients' lives, may leave. As the Standards frequently cited in this book make plain, discriminatory attitudes are not a professional option.

Most of the above examples have dealt with employment, but what is likely to engage you more as a social worker is the provision of social care, and what confuses many people is when to recognise diversity and when to regard it as irrelevant. Superficially, one might think that equality law demands that everyone is treated the same, that just as in employment, aspects of identity should be private and irrelevant. The opposite is true: treating people differently by meeting diverse needs is part of trying to create equality. For example:

- *Many patients prefer single-sex hospital wards* Providing them does not mean one sex is getting better care (unless the level of care in one is worse than the other).

- *Some residents of care homes will have religious dietary rules* Catering for vegetarian Hindus and avoiding giving *haram* food to Muslims treats people equally by treating them differently; it does no harm to non-Hindus and non-Muslims. The Arabic word *haram* means forbidden to Muslims, so pork, alcohol and (strictly speaking) prawns are *haram*, as opposed to lamb or chicken, killed according to Islamic law, which are then *halal*.

- *Documents that refer only to marriage/spouse/husband/wife ignore civil partnerships* A wide range of government documents now usually includes them, which doesn't cause any injustice to married straight people.

- *Some UK residents speak and read in other languages better than in English* Communication and information-giving only in English does not provide equal access; printing texts in other languages does not disadvantage monolingual English speakers.

- *Buildings need ramps for people in wheelchairs and induction loops so people can hear well* Not providing these things excludes people in wheelchairs; providing them doesn't exclude those who don't need them.

- *Older people are less likely to use the internet and mobile phones* Assuming everyone is familiar with these, communicating with everyone the same way, is likely to lead to unequal levels of contact.

The point of all these examples is that a wise response to diversity is *not* to treat everyone *as if* they are the same; indeed treating everyone the same can be to give them *unequal* treatment. Equality law is about recognising and allowing for diversity, and it's about breaking the link between diversity and inequality. In the employment sphere this generally means regarding aspects of identity as irrelevant criteria for appointment; in the provision of social care it frequently means the opposite.

This apparent paradox is one you have to come to terms with and negotiate. A useful phrase summing it up is *we need to discriminate between people in order not to discriminate against them.*

ACTIVITY **1.3**

Consider the need to discriminate between people so as not to discriminate against them in relation to monitoring. Do you have different responses to monitoring clients' (or fellow employees') sex and age, compared with asking about sexual orientation, religion, self-ascribed class, ethnicity or disability? If so, try to make some notes about why this is so.

Comment

Do not be surprised if you find yourself unsure how you feel about the argument above. There is a strong common-sense conviction that noticing difference somehow makes the consequences worse and that paying as little attention to it as possible is the best pathway to equitable treatment. Effective social workers have to be aware of difference to make sure it doesn't matter.

Political correctness

You might think we should just call this book *How to be a politically correct social worker*, since in any discussion of inequality and diversity the idea of politically correct language will be raised very quickly. You need to get your own responses clear. The authors of this book would say several things about so-called political correctness.

- Don't be distracted by many of the stories and accounts of what you are supposedly allowed or not allowed to say; ask, discuss, reflect and use your intelligence.

- Bear in mind that many stories of politically correct absurdities are just that – stories, which usually never happened (Gaine, 2005; Dunant, 1994).

- Consider the distracting effect of stories that seek to trivialise a concern with social injustice – it may be they are circulated to help prevent anything practical being done.

We will try to illustrate this with just two examples. Apparently it's 'not PC' to ask for black coffee because it's offensive to Black people. This is just nonsense and is shown to be so with some simple thought and reflection: in English the word black is sometimes descriptive (I'm wearing a black sweater, that's a black cat), sometimes value-laden and figurative (the black sheep of the family, it's a black day for the economy) and sometimes political (Black activists, the Black Police Officers Association). People of Caribbean, African and South Asian descent have no problem with black as a descriptive adjective; they would no sooner remove it from common usage than they would get rid of green. They may well have an issue, however, with the frequent connotation of black with bad, negative or evil (and white with the opposite, by the way). Lastly, far from disliking (capitalised) Black it is a term many have chosen, so it's certainly not going to be heard as offensive.

ACTIVITY **1.4**

Why this word has generated such anxiety is spelled out in more detail in Gaine (2005, pp81–90), but if in doubt, the test above is the one to apply. Which of the list below is offensive, and if so, what words could you substitute?

	Offensive?	Substitute, if needed
Black sheep of the family		
Black-hearted person		
Blackboard		
The Archbishop of York is a Black man		
A black mark against my name		
Young people are rarely as black as they are painted in the media		
My bank account's now in the black		
Baa baa black sheep (be careful!)		

Comment

Despite widespread mythology, there is no record at all of a local authority officially banning the singing of the nursery rhyme, though some nurseries stopped singing it out of anxiety not to offend and because they didn't think the matter through. It's interesting to consider why the popular press delight so much in spreading these myths, about which you should develop a professional scepticism.

The second example concerns people with epilepsy, apparently. The story began circulating a few years ago that the term 'brainstorm' was offensive to people with epilepsy and 'thought shower' was occasionally substituted instead. However, both the main charities who work supporting people with this condition are somewhat bemused by this; they and their members do not find the term offensive (see www.epilepsy.org.uk/press/facts/brainstorming).

No one seems to like the idea of being thought politically correct since it's seen as humourless, belonging to some kind of thought police and obsessed with mere words rather than real action. This shouldn't make us discount the importance of language; it provides a window on our thoughts, feelings, conceptions, preconceptions and prejudices (Hill and Kenyon, 2008). Nor should such anxiety diminish our awareness of how language constantly changes and the role that it can play in changing (or reinforcing) attitudes. Few people today would defend naming a sewing cotton 'nigger brown' (a name it had had since the late 1800s), yet the first protests to its manufacturer were greeted with scorn (the company renamed it sometime in the 1980s). Is referring to Down's syndrome rather than Mongol just political correctness? It took more than two decades for the former term to become standard. In London in the 1950s there was a residential School for Crippled Girls; were they right to change the name? The former Disability Rights Commission provided guidance on expressions that are likely to offend disabled people which suggested dependence or helplessness, e.g. 'deaf and dumb' as opposed to deaf without speech.

It is important that we become sensitive to those forms of language that in some way reinforce discrimination (Thompson, 2003, p153). There are subtle ways in which language can reflect and reinforce differences or inequalities, and sensitivity to this is an alternative to doctrinaire and unexplained lists of taboo words on the one hand and complacency on the other.

ACTIVITY **1.5**

Diversity challenge

Imagine that one evening you're invited out with a group of old school or family friends to a local pub quiz. Since you have been on your social work course you have begun to feel awkward and uncomfortable regarding certain aspects of the language they use and the jokes they tell. You find aspects of their language discriminatory, homophobic, sexist and derogatory and their jokes are really not that funny. You enjoy their company and don't really want to end your friendship, but having learnt about discrimination at university you have since changed some beliefs and let previous ones go.

- *What reactions may prevent you from dealing with this situation?*

- *What strategies and language might you adopt to constructively challenge certain statements you find discriminatory and offensive?*

Comment

Common reactions may be to avoid challenging your friends' language altogether, or to minimise, trivialise or disregard such language as irrelevant or unimportant. These reactions, common though they are, prevent us from continuing to develop and learn.

Other responses may be to:

- make your excuses to stop meeting with your friends;

- talk the situation through separately with one of the group asking what their views are, not just about their language but the reactions it evokes in you;

- divert the conversation onto another topic when it drifts into discriminatory or derogatory language;

- tackle the issue head-on with the group but rehearse what you might say and prepare for what their responses might be. Maybe you feel that some of your friends could come to see things differently.

Whatever your response may be it is worth critically reflecting upon why you chose one response over another. Is it to do with gaps in your learning, or your current level of skills, knowledge or experience which may prevent you confidently challenging discrimination, or is it to do with or uncertainty about your values?

The art of elegant challenging

Thompson (2009) refers to the notion of *elegant challenging* which aims to get your point across without alienating or antagonising the individual(s) being challenged. An overzealous approach may not result in a positive change but create a hostile, defensive, tense reaction or even be interpreted as an oppressive act itself. Elegant challenging aims to initiate a change in attitude and behaviour without being too confrontational. This issue is taken up again in the final chapter.

Different kinds of struggle

At the time of writing in early 2010, British equality law is in the final stages of revision before a new act is passed. This has involved integrating previous laws about race, sex and disability discrimination into a coherent framework that includes religion, sexual orientation and age. It will cover discrimination in employment and the provision of services of all kinds, and for some aspects of diversity it will protect people against hate speech or writing. This new legal framework has partly come about as an attempt to tidy up existing legislation in line with changing public attitudes and partly in response to trends in Europe harmonising equality laws.

Earlier, we mentioned social class, which has been included within the new law as 'socio-economic status' though in practice it will be covered less than gender, age, race, religion, sexual orientation and disability. Social class is not quite the same kind of thing as the other aspects of diversity. It's much harder to define and in relation to many of the factors that contribute to a person's class (education, earnings, accent, housing) some people change their social class during their lifetime and indeed try hard to do so. Where class might be comparable to the other aspects of diversity is when it is regarded as a fixed quality, a kind of stain that cannot be washed out in the same way that a Chinese person might be considered unchangeably different, or a woman, however demonstrably capable, is regarded as irredeemably unsuitable for senior management. Thus a well qualified and capable person with a working-class childhood, perhaps revealed by accent, might experience prejudice on the irrelevant basis of their origins. However, with reference to the discussion of relevance earlier, insofar as education is a component of class it's hard to argue against it being a relevant criterion in getting many jobs, and while salary according to one's level or status in an organisation is part of what creates classes this is not unjust in the same way as paying a woman less just because she's female.

With social class what's likely to happen in the new law is that there may be a duty on public bodies to consider what effect their overall strategies have on reducing inequalities that arise from socio-economic disadvantage; they will not be answerable for their day-to-day delivery of services as they are with regard to race, for example.

The chapter on social class makes reference to political and economic history, and to Karl Marx. A good deal of the twentieth century revolved around the notion that class inequalities and the resulting conflicts were the fundamental forces driving historical change. The main political parties in most European countries reflect this, the British Labour Party very obviously signalling in its name and many of its policies a concern to reduce inequalities based upon class. (This is not to say that their main rival, the Conservatives, think it is unimportant, but they have historically taken a different approach.) It may seem ironic, therefore, that class is covered much less by equality legislation, so we need to consider why this is so.

The reason, we would argue, is that because it is seen as so fundamental to our social structure it is not amenable to legislation in the same way. Depending on one's point of view, class represents either a fundamental injustice whereby the work of many is exploited by a powerful few, or a reasonably just and fair way of distributing benefits and goods according to talent and effort. Either way, it can't be changed by a mere law: it's too fundamental.

Taking the second view first, differentials between the highest and lowest pay could, in principle, be reduced; wealth could be massively taxed and blocked from being passed between generations, but pay differences would remain and few would regard them as inherently unjust in the way they might with gender or disability. There are not many who would argue the brain surgeon should receive the same pay as the hospital cleaner, largely because of the point discussed earlier – relevance. It is relevant to their pay levels that while both are important jobs, one requires many years of effort and training and skills that not everyone has. It carries greater job satisfaction but also greater responsibility, so while the size of the pay gap is debatable there's not much doubt there needs to be a gap. The argument about class inequality becomes not whether there should be any inequality, but how we ensure fair chances to become economically unequal to one another.

Returning to the first (Marxist-derived) position that class divisions are fundamentally unjust because undue economic and hence political power is held by a powerful few, this is an analysis that is used to explain the chronic persistence of class inequalities (discussed further in the chapter on class). By this analysis it would be impossible significantly to erode differences because the system depends on them. It would be like proposing a bee colony without a queen and the corresponding thousands of worker bees: the answer isn't a bit more honey for the workers but a new social system. The fact that we can't imagine this new system makes a different Marxist point, that our thinking is so constrained by the hegemonic ideology of what we know (or are allowed to know) that we can't think outside the hive.

Similar Marxist analysis has been applied both to racism and to sexism. For both, it is argued, we do not simply have an unfortunate historic legacy of old ideas that have yet to fade away: both forms of inequality are profitable. It serves the interests of the capitalist class to have a supply of workers they can turn on and off as required – a reserve army of labour: immigrants and women at home, both of whom are ideologically constructed as inferior so they can be treated as such, with fewer employment (or even residence) rights, lower pay, and so on. For class, race and gender, the struggle has mainly been about a politics of redistribution, primarily redistribution of economic resources but also the related power, and as regards the starkest, most obvious injustices of ascribed status they have had some success.

For older people, disabled people, lesbians and gay men, and those with a range of faiths outside the historic British norm, there has been instead largely a politics of emancipation and recognition (Butler, 1998; Fraser, 1998). It is hard to argue that the marginalisation of some religious groups or discrimination against gay men served the economic needs of capitalism. It may have done at times (by policing strict gender boundaries), but there are other less tortuous explanations and besides, being more often childless, lesbian and gay couples frequently have more spending power, the so-called pink pound. Similarly, the ways in which disabled people or older people are regarded are not in any obvious way related to exploiting their labour power, older people as a whole having greater wealth than younger people because of more years accumulating property and savings. Thus the kind of equality sought by those of various faiths, lesbians, gay men and bisexuals, disabled people and older people, while certainly involving freedom from unjust job discrimination and hence a full range of economic opportunities, also involves cultural and social recognition, the recognition of their full humanity.

This distinction should not be taken in too absolute a way, but the point is to recognise the different dimensions of inequality. It is sometimes mainly economic, and the struggles in someone's life that may entail the support of a social worker may stem largely from low pay, unemployment or poverty (see case studies in the chapter on class). At other times a client's life may be limited by entirely social and cultural factors, such as being viewed as childlike or asexual because of old age.

The law and different inequalities

It was noted above that we are in the midst of harmonising several different laws that have been passed in Britain over a forty-year period. The most important of these are:

- Equal Pay Act 1970;
- Sex Discrimination Act 1975 plus the Sex Discrimination (Amendment) Act 1985 and Gender Reassignment Regulations 1999;
- Race Relations Act 1976 and Race Relations (Amendment) Act 2000;
- Disability Discrimination Acts 1995 and 2005;
- Human Rights Act 1998;
- Employment Equality (Sexual Orientation) Regulations 2003;
- Employment Equality (Religion or Belief) Regulations 2003;
- European Commission Goods and Services Directive 2004/113;
- Disability Equality Duty 2006;
- Equality Act 2006;
- Employment Equality (Age) Regulations 2006;
- Gender Equality Duty 2007.

As suggested earlier, this is partly motivated by harmonising treaties across the EU, but the case for integrating the laws into a common approach is also made by the evidence of persisting inequality.

- Despite progress since 1997 to reduce the gender pay gap women still earn, on average, 22.6 per cent less per hour than men.

- Less academically able but better off children overtake more able poorer children at school by the age of six.

- The gap between the employment rate of disabled people and the overall employment rate has decreased from 34.5 per cent to 26.3 per cent since 1998, but disabled people are still more than twice as likely to be unemployed than non-disabled people.

- If you are from an ethnic minority, you were 17.9 per cent less likely to find work in 1997 than a white person. The difference is still 13 per cent.

- One in five older people are unsuccessful in getting quotations for motor, travel or car hire insurances.

- Six out of ten lesbian and gay school children experience homophobic bullying and many contemplate suicide as a result.

(Government Equalities Office, 2009)

The first step towards an integrated approach was in 2007, merging the separate commissions for disability, race and gender into the Equality and Human Rights Commission (EHRC). (The Disability Rights Commission (DRC), the Commission for Racial Equality (CRE) and the Equal Opportunities Commission (EOC) no longer exist). The next stage, a Single Equality Act, will protect the groups we are concerned with in this book from various kinds of discrimination and impose a duty on public bodies to promote equality and combat discrimination. Some additional features may be:

- using procurement (purchasing services) to improve equality;

- banning age discrimination outside the workplace;

- introducing a requirement for gender pay and equality reports from organisations;

- extending the scope for using positive action, e.g. encouraging employers to create a more diverse workforce and helping under-represented groups to compete for promotion;

- protecting carers from discrimination;

- protecting breastfeeding mothers;

- banning discrimination in private members' clubs;

- strengthening protection from discrimination for disabled people;

- extending the circumstance in which a person is protected against discrimination, harassment or victimisation because of a protected characteristic;

- strengthening employment tribunals to make recommendations in discrimination cases which apply to the whole workforce.

The Bill is expected to become law in late spring 2010 and should come into force by the autumn, with the general public duty following about a year later, but none of this is certain. Each chapter in the book makes some reference the key principles of the law as it stands.

Embarking on the rest of the book

ACTIVITY 1.6

Diversity personal reflection plan

As part of this book's learning strategy, all the authors will encourage you to reflect upon each chapter in terms of how the things you have learnt will change the way you think and act towards others who are different to you in both your personal and professional lives. After each chapter, therefore, we'd encourage you to ask the following questions.

What has this chapter helped me to learn about myself with regard to:

- *my beliefs?*
- *my attitudes?*
- *my values?*
- *my knowledge of others?*
- *my behaviour?*
- *my use of language?*
- *my responsibilities as a social worker?*
- *the way I see the world?*

How do I need to change in order to become:

- *more sensitive?*
- *less prejudicial?*
- *less discriminatory?*
- *better able to deal with individuals according to their needs?*

If I were to change one thing about the way I act as a result of reading this chapter what would it be ...?

(Adapted from Clements and Spinks, 2008)

C H A P T E R   S U M M A R Y

This chapter has introduced key distinctions and concepts and spelled out their relevance for social workers. It has also made some comparisons between different aspects of diversity and inequality. Some legal as well as professional obligations have been outlined, as has some guidance on the troublesome issue of appropriate language.

Bagilhole, B (2009) *Understanding equal opportunities and diversity: The social differentiations and intersections of equality*. Bristol: The Policy Press.

An up-to-date and useful guide that navigates clearly through the social policy, institutional and legal maze of equal opportunities and diversity.

Dalrymple, J and Burke, B (1995) *Anti-oppressive practice: Social care and the law*. Buckingham: Open University Press.

An important text which explores the essential elements of anti-oppressive theory, power, legislation and social work practice.

Dominelli, L (2008) *Anti-Racist social work*. 3rd edition. Basingstoke: Palgrave Macmillan.

A revised, highly influential and comprehensive text which provides case studies and practice guidance.

Hill, H and Kenyon, R (2008) *Promoting equality and diversity: A practitioner's guide*. Oxford: Oxford University Press.

A useful and accessible legal framework guide for practitioners and lawyers.

Hills, J, Sefton, T and Stewart, K (eds) (2009) *Towards a more equal society: Poverty, inequality and policy since 1997*. Bristol: The Policy Press and The Joseph Rowntree Foundation.

A new and very readable account of recent developments.

Thompson, N (2003). *Promoting equality: Challenging discrimination and oppression*. 2nd edition. Basingstoke: Palgrave Macmillan.

An essential text to aid all practitioners to understand discrimination, oppression and diversity.

www.equalities.gov.uk

The Government Equalities Office (GEO) has responsibility for equality strategy and legislation and takes the lead on issues relating to women, sexual orientation and transgender equality matters.

www.equalityhumanrights.com

An independent UK statutory body (created in 2007) to help eliminate discrimination, enforce equality laws, reduce inequality and protect human rights and to build good relations aims to ensure society is built upon fairness and respect.

www.jrf.org.uk

The Joseph Rowntree Foundation seeks solutions to social problems and monitors and researches poverty and social exclusion.

www.runnymedetrust.org

Promotes a successful multi-ethnic Britain in the spirit of civic friendship, shared identity and a common sense of belonging. The Trust publishes useful practitioner handbooks, briefing papers and research reports.

Chapter 2
Gender

Barbara Thompson

ACHIEVING A SOCIAL WORK DEGREE

This chapter will help you meet the following National Occupational Standards.

Key Role 1: Prepare for, and work with individuals, families, carers, groups and communities to assess their needs and circumstances.

- Prepare for social work contact and involvement.
- Work with individuals, families, carers, groups and communities to help them make informed decisions.

Key Role 2: Plan, carry out, review and evaluate social work practice, with individuals, families, carers, groups, communities and other professionals.

- Interact with individuals, families, carers, groups and communities to achieve change and development and to improve life opportunities.

Key Role 3: Support individuals to represent their needs, views and circumstances.

- Advocate with, and on behalf of, individuals, families, carers, groups and communities.

Key Role 6: Demonstrate professional competence in social work practice.

- Research, analyse, evaluate and use current knowledge of best social work practice.

It will also introduce you to the following academic standards as set out in the social work subject benchmark statement.

5.1.1 Social work services, service users and carers.

- Explanations of the links between definitional processes contributing to social differences (for example, social class, gender, ethnic differences, age, sexuality and religious belief) to the problems of inequality and differential need faced by service users.
- The nature of social work services in a diverse society (with particular reference to concepts such as prejudice, interpersonal, institutional and structural discrimination, empowerment and anti-discriminatory practices).

5.1.3 Values and ethics.

- The moral concepts of rights, responsibility, freedom, authority and power inherent in the practice of social workers as moral and statutory agents.

5.5.3 Analysis and synthesis.

- Assess the merits of contrasting theories, explanations, research, policies and procedures.
- Critically analyse and take account of the impact of inequality and discrimination in work with people in particular contexts and problem situations.

Introduction

This chapter will ask you to reflect upon the effect that your gender may have on the way you carry out your role, either as a beginner or more senior social worker. In particular, it will ask you to consider the ways that your gender identity may influence not only the ways in which you view your role, but also the ways in which you may be seen and the expectations that others may have of you. For example, historically, the 'caring professions' such as teaching, nursing and social work have been seen as suitable work for women as they were, or in the eyes of some people are, linked to notions of women's traditional 'mothering' role within the family (Acker and Feuerverger, 1996). Similarly doing 'emotional labour' is more often associated with women than with men. As Smethurst points out:

> *Empathy, sensitivity and the ability to read and manage others' emotions are skills and qualities typically associated with women.*

> (Smethurst, 2007, p97)

Although notions of femininity and masculinity can be debated, long-established cultural stereotypes run deep and men and women and who enter the caring professions may be regarded in different ways from one another (Christie, 2001). All of us will have deeply embedded views as to how we think men/boys and women/girls should behave, whether we realise this or not, and it is important for all those with a commitment to diversity and equality work to explore these ideas: unless we understand these issues ourselves we cannot engage in good practice. This chapter will explore how long-standing stereotypes about men and women have become embedded in notions about what is 'proper' male and female behaviour and how these convictions have shaped policy and practice in social work (and in other fields too).

Across all societies men and women behave differently in some ways. However, just as importantly, more recent research shows that there are also many instances where men and women and boys and girls behave in very similar ways, and that there are many differences between what different women do and what different men do as well as many similarities (Mirza, 1997; Francis, 1999, 2006). However, before investigating these gender issues further, it is important to understand what the terms sex and gender mean as they are often, wrongly, used interchangeably.

In the first section of the chapter we will examine these key terms, as well as gender equality and gender role. Next the issue of gender equality will be placed within a historical framework in order to see where some of the lingering stereotypes related to men and women and boys and girls have originated. After this we will explore some of the more common theories about gender and see how these have changed over time, and finally we will examine how we construct our own gender identities. It is the case that some people in the twenty-first century think that gender equality is no longer a problem and it is quite common to hear young people remark that gender is a dead issue that belonged to their parents' generation (Coffey and Delamont, 2000). This is particularly the case in relation to the perceived educational and assumed career success of girls as media headlines have whipped up a 'moral panic' about the perceived underachievement of boys (Epstein, et al., 1998; Thompson, 2006). Headlines that began to appear from the mid-1990s such as *Girls doing well while boys feel neglected* do not take into account the fact that, as with most things, these issues are not as straightforward as they may at first appear and that not all males are underachieving and not all females are being successful (Skelton and Francis, 2009).

It is most important that all those engaged in social work have a good understanding of issues of gender equality in order to ensure that those in their care are treated in a fair and equitable way within a genuinely inclusive environment. This can be quite challenging as the process of examining or re-examining your own thoughts may cause you to question some of your preconceived ideas.

ACTIVITY **2.1**

Do you think that males and females should behave in any particular ways?

Write down some words that you think apply to girls/women ... and then to boys/men.

Ask people of a similar age group as yourself what they think.

Now repeat this exercise with some older women and men. Are there any differences in what different genders think? Are there differences between what different age groups think?

Comment

It will be no surprise to you that you get different responses, but it's worth reflecting that gender is an aspect of diversity we all know about, we all have experience of. Different views and approaches to diversity (and inequality) do not necessarily come about because of unfamiliarity.

Understanding the terms

Sometimes the terms sex and gender are confused with one another. It is important that professionals have a clear understanding of terms such as sex, gender assignment, gender identity and gender role. *Sex* refers to matters of biology and a person's sex is usually taken to be a matter of bodily form and hormonal configurations. *Gender assignment* is usually given at birth, although as Paechter reminds us:

> ... we all assign gender, all the time to the people that we meet; we do this so unconsciously that we only notice ourselves doing it when we make a 'mistake' when someone presents themselves to us so ambiguously for us to have to weigh up the possibilities. Gender assignment is usually, though not always, aligned with (some definition of) biological sex.
>
> (Paechter, 2001, p47)

Gender identity refers to the way that people feel about their own gender, whether they are male, female or transgender (Kessler and McKenna, 1978). You cannot make assumptions about how people feel about their gender identity unless you ask them, which may not be appropriate. *Gender role* refers to a set of behaviours that are tradition-ally assigned to particular genders and may vary according to culture and across time. For example, as Skelton and Francis point out:

> *… young girls learn how to be a girl by receiving approval for feminine traits such as caring, gentleness and helpfulness while young boys learn that they are expected to be boisterous, rough and energetic.*
>
> (Skelton and Francis, 2003, p12)

It may well be the case that gender roles are not as essentialist (all females do this and all males do that) as they used to be. For example, it is highly unlikely that middle-class girls will be found sitting and sewing in the parlour on a Sunday afternoon as they may have been expected to do in Victorian times, but it is also true that gender stereotypes are very persistent.

Placing gender inequality within an historical framework

It helps our understanding of why there were, and in some cases still are, different expec-tations of what females and males should do if we look back into history. Over time the lives of girls have, for the most part, been a preparation for their future roles as wives and mothers and this affected how they were treated as children in relation to boys. The ideology of female educational provision has been that it should be both inferior to, and different from, that provided for men. As Kamm states:

> *For the vast majority of girls of all classes, marriage was the real goal. If a girl stayed at home under her mother's eye, if she went to a village school, or boarded in a convent, or with a noble family, her prime consideration was to find a suitable husband.*
>
> (Kamm, 1965, p28)

Lewis describes the idealised notion of womanhood revealed by such Victorian writers as Ruskin and Coventry Patmore:

> *A woman's fundamental task was to create a haven of peace, beauty and security for their husbands and children. The home was to be a sanctuary in which the wife reigned as guardian 'angel' in the words of Patmore, or as a Queen in the imagery of Ruskin.*
>
> (Lewis, 1984, p81)

This association of women with a *caring script* (Acker and Feuerverger, 1996) and with roles as wives and mothers within the domestic sphere has historically become formalised in policies related to the sort of upbringing that girls should have and the sort of jobs that women should do.

Enshrining gender difference within social policy

The curricula of elementary schools throughout history were to fit girls for life. Girls' education of whatever class, whether undertaken by mother, school or governess, was rooted in the domestic. As adult life was sex-segregated, it was only natural to devise an educational system that fitted children to that system (Arnot, 1986). At least until the First World War most girls in Britain received an important part of their education in the home and as Purvis informs us:

> *All women were expected to conform to an ideal of domesticity, which disapproved of working women and which located feminine virtue in a domestic and familial setting.*
>
> (Purvis, 1995, p107)

Dyhouse (1981, p103) argues that that there was a strongly held belief that sending girls to school would encourage academic aspirations which would turn their attention away from domestic duties and attachment to the home. Official policy reinforced a separate and sexist education, which for girls was centred on preparing them for wife- and motherhood. For example, the Norwood Report argued:

> *The grounds for including domestic subjects in the curricula are ... firstly that knowledge of such subjects is necessary equipment for all girls as potential makers of homes.*
>
> (Committee of the Secondary Schools Examination Council, 1943, p127)

The Plowden Report (DES, 1967) provided an emphasis on individualised learning and established child-centred approaches to education. Although focusing educational provision on the demands of the individual seems designed to establish equality of opportunity, it could be argued that child-centred approaches mean that more teacher time is given to those who are more dominant in the classroom, usually boys.

The passing of the Sex Discrimination Act in 1975 saw the enshrining of boys' and girls' entitlement to the same curriculum in law and the National Curriculum which came into being in 1988 ensured that girls and boys took the same core subjects for the first time. It could be assumed therefore that gender discrimination in education would be a thing of the past. However, the lingering stereotypes attached to traditional gender roles mean that teachers and other professionals may continue to treat girls and boys differently. For example, not that long ago I observed a lesson in a primary school where the children were asked to construct a shelter for dinosaurs; the task was therefore the same for both genders. However, the response of the teacher to the children's work was very different depending on their gender. When a boy brought out his shelter the discussion centred on the most effective shape which could be used make a strong roof. When a girl brought out her work, she was told that she had *decorated the shelter very nicely*.

So far this section of the chapter has concentrated on educational policy and practice because, as all children go to school, the messages that they receive there about what are regarded as appropriate gendered behaviours and roles are powerful. However, social work has its own policies that reflect stereotyped gendered assumptions. Smethurst (2007, p96) draws our attention to the *Curtis Report* (Care of Children Committee, 1946, para. 446) which noted that women brought special feminine qualities of engaging with others and were able *to set both children and adults at their ease*. Although this report was written a long time ago, people working in the caring professions are still expected, in a *quasi-maternal manner to care for and care about others* (Acker and Feuerverger, 1996, p401).

ACTIVITY **2.2**

- *How much do you think the 'caring script' continues to influence the life/educational choices of girls and boys today?*

- *What made you decide to become a social worker? What were the dominant influences?*

- *Think about your own early life. Did you notice boys and girls being encouraged to respond to emotional situations in different ways?*

CASE STUDY

Emma

Emma is a young woman who works as a clerk in a firm of solicitors. Her elderly mother has just come to live with her as Emma is keen that she should not have to be put into a home. Her mother requires help with getting up in the morning and dressing herself, and needs her meals providing. This means that Emma has to get up very early in the morning to prepare sandwiches for her mother's lunch and to begin to get her up. Helpers organised though Social Services come to help with washing and dressing in the morning, but often do not arrive before the time that Emma should leave for work. As she does not like to leave her mother on her own before she is up and dressed this means that she is often late for work and her employers are beginning to complain. Social Services have also just told Emma that because of staffing shortages they can no longer provide help at the weekends and Emma is becoming exhausted. She is also aware that a male colleague who is in a similar situation to herself has help arranged through Social Services for attendance at the weekend as well as early morning help.

As the social worker attached to Emma's mother what concerns would you have? What gendered discourses do you think might be in play that might account for the differential treatment accorded to Emma and her male colleague? How would you act in order to take some of the pressure off Emma and to ensure that her mother gets the best possible care?

Comment

You may or may not think this contrast in treatment unlikely. We would contend that it's perfectly possible, not because of any deliberate actions but through a chain of unexamined assumptions. This is how diversity can be translated into disadvantage.

Doing emotional labour: Men and women in social work

Just as stereotypes related to caring, sensitivity and emotion attach themselves to women, so there are others that are traditionally associated with men such as being the breadwinner, being tough and being unemotional ('boys don't cry'). However, just as the stereotypes attached to being female can be challenged, so can those attached to being male. As Connell informs us:

Historians and anthropologists have shown that there is no one pattern of masculinity that is found everywhere. Different cultures and different periods of history construct masculinity differently. For example some cultures make heroes of soldiers, and make violence the ultimate test of masculinity; others look at [...] soldiering with disdain and regard soldiering as contemptible ... Typically some masculinities are more honoured than others ... The form of masculinity which is culturally dominant in a given setting is called 'hegemonic' masculinity.

(Connell, 2006, pp20–1)

Just as in the other caring professions, the women in social work far outnumber men (Perry and Cree, 2003). This may mean that some men working in a predominantly female profession could feel uncomfortable, or it may mean that male social workers, because of stereotypes related to males such as lack of emotion on the one hand and technical competence on the other (Smethurst, 2007), will quickly gain promotion. Acker and Feuerverger point out that:

In these fields a gendered division of labour occurs between large numbers of female workers and a smaller elite cadre of male managers.

(Acker and Feuerverger, 1996, p406)

However, recently several critiques have emerged about common-sense assumptions in relation to the caring professions. For example, the fact that women have been seen as naturally suited to these professions has served to disguise the potential for exploitation in terms of low pay. Similarly the increased workload caused as a result of increased bureaucratisation throughout the public sector (Clarke and Newman, 1997) helps us to understand why (mainly women) workers might exhaust themselves trying to do the intensified job conscientiously. Most notably, there is a growing recognition that diversity between men and men and diversity between women and women is not sufficiently recognised, and as a result both men and women may be trapped in restrictive stereotypes (Connell, 2006). It has even been questioned by some whether social work is in fact a particularly feminised profession (Bagilhole and Cross, 2006).

Nonetheless, it is a fact that social work will lead you into situations where you will have to deal with people who may exhibit powerful emotions such as anxiety, distress or possibly aggression. Your gender may, however unfairly, mean that people will expect you to deal with these situations in stereotyped ways. For example, it may be that, if you are male, neither your clients nor your superiors will expect you to be particularly emotional, or they may expect you to deal successfully with aggressive clients. Conversely, if you are a female you may be expected to work with very young children or with what are perceived as women's issues. In addition, it may be the case that male social workers may feel that they have to bottle up their feelings and distress more than their female colleagues.

ACTIVITY 2.3

- *How would you describe the hegemonic masculinity in aspects of British culture and why may this be problematic for some male social workers?*

- *Do you think that social workers should be allocated different work according to their gender?*

Comment

As elsewhere in this book, you will probably be thinking about potential conflicts between your own views, those of other colleagues (male and female) and clients and their families. Negotiating these is an inescapable part of the job.

CASE STUDY

Tom and Mr Jones

You are a senior social worker and have just had Tom, a young social worker, assigned to your team. You have sent Tom round to see Mr Jones, an elderly man who has just been widowed. You are unsure as to Mr Jones' needs and have asked Tom to pay a preliminary visit to make a judgement about what support is needed. Tom returns to the office obviously upset and saying that Mr Jones would not let him in, saying that he wasn't going to discuss his private affairs with a young man. He had also implied that being a social worker wasn't a suitable job for a man. You are reluctant to take Tom away from this case, but need to consider what you will do to try and build a working relationship between the two men.

The persistence of stereotypes

So far we have spent a lot of time considering how males and females have been constructed as different over time, even though more recent research has challenged these ideas (Acker and Feuerverger, 1996; Francis, 1999; Connell, 2006). For some people, even in the twenty-first century, the notion that males and females remain different categories of human beings is so familiar that they take it for granted. For example, pink and blue baby clothes are still manufactured and bought for the different sexes. The media is very influential in promoting these stereotypes. If you watch and listen to the advertisements on television, or look at children's toy catalogues, you will find that the messages given to girls and boys about supposedly proper toys and activities for them to engage in are not that dissimilar from those of earlier generations, as this nineteenth-century verse shows:

> *Mamma and Miss Ann*
> *Mamma. Go and buy a toy, Ann.*
> *Ann. Can I buy a gun?*
> *Mamma. A gun is not fit for you, Ann.*
> *Ann. Why is a gun not fit for me?*
> *Mamma. A gun is fit only for a boy.*
> *Ann. May I buy a top?*
> *Mamma. No, but you may buy a mop.*

(Arnold, 1969, p19, cited in Madoc-Jones and Coates, 1996)

It is interesting to consider whether a similar conversation would occur nowadays and there is some evidence that, far from disappearing, these stereotypes remain firmly entrenched. For example, Browne (2004) notes that young children see superhero roles as almost exclusively male, and it is overwhelmingly boys who engage in superhero play. As we have also noted, trapping boys and girls within stereotypes can be both limiting and damaging.

ACTIVITY **2.4**

Consider what you think about some common-sense gendered assumptions that still exist today, for example pink for girls and blue for boys.

Ask yourself what it is like for young people who do not want to follow traditional roles, for example boys who do not like football, or girls that do.

Comment
It is worth examining some influential theories related to gender relations in order both to understand and be able to challenge some of these ideas.

Some important perspectives and theories related to gender equality

The nature/nurture debate – biology or culture?

Gender issues tend to arouse strong feelings and many of these are related to people's standpoint on what they think is the nature of gender. By this I mean whether they think that gender difference is based on biological differences and is therefore natural and unchanging or whether they think that gender identity is socially constructed and is likely to change over time (or a mixture of the two). This is called the nature/nurture debate and it is very long running and hotly contested.

Some thoughts about innate gender difference
Evolutionary psychologists argue that gender differences simply reflect biological differences. This would argue that we are all predestined to certain gendered behaviours that are fixed and inevitable and will not change (Birkhead, 2001). These theorists maintain that this is why men often respond to certain problems by only using one side of their brain while women tend to use both sides. This leads on to notions that men tend to use a linear approach to problem solving while women use a more holistic approach and thus men are found more often in scientific and mathematical jobs and women in the arts, humanities and caring professions. However, as Francis informs us:

> *Neuroscientific evidence has shown that the brain develops through social interaction, and as a result of environmental/circumstantial factors.*
>
> (Francis, 2006, p9)

On the other hand, studies such as those of Gerhardt (2004) suggest that brain differences between men and women may be caused by their different experiences. For example, if boys are given cars and construction kits, they are more likely to develop those parts of the brain that are used in playing with those toys such as spatial awareness.

You might like to reflect for a moment on where you think you stand in relation to the nature/nurture debate and whether this might affect the way you deal with boys and girls, men and women.

Socially constructed gender roles

In contrast to those theorists who believe that gender differences are innate there is an opposing body of thought that believes that society has a powerful role in influencing how we construct our identities (Francis and Skelton, 2005; Thompson, 2006). For example, as we have seen earlier, historically, the ideology of domesticity has always shaped the lives of girls and women; however, with the coming of the First World War there was an enormous increase in female employment outside the home as women were encouraged to take on jobs vacated by men at war. Although in peacetime there was pressure for women to return to the home (Lewis, 1984) with the coming of the Second World War, women were once again encouraged to take up work and this time, at the end of the war, many fewer women gave up paid employment. The argument here is that if gender roles are biologically determined, then they would not change in accordance with societal demands, nor would women resist returning to 'their place'.

Sex role theory

Sex role theory argues that gender identity is learnt by children through institutions such as the family, the school, the peer group and the media (Sharpe, 1976; Stanworth, 1981). Sex role theory was prevalent in feminist studies of the 1970s, 1980s and early 1990s and focused on providing girls and boys with non-gender stereotyped images in textbooks, non-gender stereotyped activities in the classroom and in careers advice. Activities based on sex role theory are still to be found in contemporary classrooms and have met with some success in that they have been useful in marking a shift away from seeing gender as something biological to something socially constructed. However, commentators such as Skelton and Francis (2003) and Thompson (2006) argue that simply providing children with a variety of different activities and hoping that they will engage with them is not enough. Thompson (2006, p104) refers to Davies' (1989) work with young children and fairy tales where children were given alternative images of princesses who were assertive, resourceful and problem solving. However, the children in Davies' study did not 'hear' these alternative messages because they did not fit with their own constructions of what a princess should be and as a result thought that these non-traditional images meant that these were not proper princesses. Skelton and Francis argue that sex role theory sees children as *passive recipients as to what society expects and does not account for difference between females and difference between males. Nor does it account for the fact that people may be active in constructing their own identities* (Skelton and Francis, 2003, p14).

Gender relational theory

Gender relational theory argues that how people create their identities is situational and relational and is affected by such issues as class background, ethnicity, age and life experiences. In other words, we become who we are through the situations that we encounter and through social interactions. This theory accounts for the fact that not all females and males behave in stereotyped ways. For example, not all females are quiet, unassertive and sexually reserved and not all males like cars, football, are boisterous and are good at putting up shelves. Commentators who support the notion of gender relational theory argue that those who work with children should encourage them to understand that there are many acceptable ways of being a male and many acceptable ways of being a female. As MacNaughton argues:

> *Identity is formed and reformed in interaction with others. Re-shaping children's gendered identity requires considerable child–child and child–adult interaction ...*
> *One aim of this interaction is to expand children's ways of seeing and doing gender.*

> (MacNaughton, 2000, p23)

CASE STUDY

Molly

Molly is 16 and academically very able. She lives with her father who is a single parent and who has just gained custody of Molly and her younger brother and sister. Although her father is aware that her school thinks Molly could, and should, go to university, he has made it very clear that he is very keen for her to leave school and take care of the younger children. Molly loves her dad and wants to help him but she is desperately keen to go to university and train in medicine. As the family's social worker how will you help to resolve the tensions in the household and help Molly to fulfil her ambition?

Gender, the law and you

This chapter has sought to give you an overview of some of the key issues related to gender issues with particular reference to social work. However, a commitment to gender equality is not only good practice, it is a matter of law. The Sex Discrimination Act was passed in the UK in 1975 and along with the Race Relations Act of 1976 was partly inspired by the civil rights movement which started in the 1960s in the USA (Skelton and Francis, 2009). The Sex Discrimination Act gave girls and boys the entitlement to have the same curriculum in law; however, as I have noted elsewhere (Thompson, 2006), education was reluctant to engage with the Act. As we have seen earlier in this chapter, schools remained (remain?) patriarchal institutions which tend to uphold the status quo. However, the Sex Discrimination Act was amended by the Equality Act in 2006 and, following that, the Gender Equality Duty came into force on 6 April 2007. This differs from previous gender equality legislation in three main ways.

- There is a requirement for public authorities to be proactive rather than reactive.

- The requirement is to promote equality, not just avoid discrimination.

- Due regard must be paid to unlawful discrimination and harassment against transsexual people.

(www.ecu.ac.uk)

Therefore as a professional working in social work you not only need the desire and commitment to implement gender equity in your practice, you have a duty under the law. This requires you to be active in working to eliminate gender inequality wherever you might encounter it in the workplace.

C H A P T E R   S U M M A R Y

Making a difference

This chapter has explored some of the key notions related to gender equality over time. It has explained some important terminology and investigated where traditional gender stereotypes may have originated, noting how resistant these stereotypes are. It has considered some of the changing theories and legislation related to the gender agenda and asked you not only to consider where you position yourself in relation to these debates but also to reflect upon how your own stance impacts on your job in social work. As you have taken the decision to train as a social worker, hopefully it can be assumed that you already have a commitment to issues of equality and social justice, although some of you will have found this chapter more challenging than others. However, no matter where you are in the journey we all make in understanding gender relations, it is important to be aware that what you do as an individual is crucial. Understanding and challenging inequality can be difficult, time-consuming and stressful but having the commitment to do so is vital.

FURTHER READING

Christie, A (ed.) (2001) *Men in social work*. Basingstoke: Palgrave.

This book provides an accessible overview of key debates in social work.

Skeggs, B (2002) *Formations of class and gender: Becoming respectable*. London: Sage.

This book offers an illuminating explanation of how identities are formed and, in particular, how the 'caring self' is constructed.

Chapter 3
Sexual orientation

Chris Gaine

A C H I E V I N G   A   S O C I A L   W O R K   D E G R E E

This chapter will help you meet the following National Occupational Standards.

Key Role 1: Prepare for, and work with individuals, families, carers, groups and communities to assess their needs and circumstances.

- Prepare for social work contact and involvement.
- Work with individuals, families, carers, groups and communities to help them make informed decisions.

Key Role 2: Plan, carry out, review and evaluate social work practice, with individuals, families, carers, groups, communities and other professionals.

- Interact with individuals, families, carers, groups and communities to achieve change and development and to improve life opportunities.

Key Role 3: Support individuals to represent their needs, views and circumstances.

- Advocate with, and on behalf of, individuals, families, carers, groups and communities.

Key Role 6: Demonstrate professional competence in social work practice.

- Research, analyse, evaluate and use current knowledge of best social work practice.

It will also introduce you to the following academic standards as set out in the social work subject benchmark statement.

5.1.1 Social work services, service users and carers.

- Explanations of the links between definitional processes contributing to social differences (for example, social class, gender, ethnic differences, age, sexuality and religious belief) to the problems of inequality and differential need faced by service users.
- The nature of social work services in a diverse society (with particular reference to concepts such as prejudice, interpersonal, institutional and structural discrimination, empowerment and anti-discriminatory practices).

5.1.3 Values and ethics.

The moral concepts of rights, responsibility, freedom, authority and power inherent in the practice of social workers as moral and statutory agents.

5.5.3 Analysis and synthesis.

- Assess the merits of contrasting theories, explanations, research, policies and procedures.
- Critically analyse and take account of the impact of inequality and discrimination in work with people in particular contexts and problem situations.

Introduction

Until 1967 it was illegal for men to be gay, or at least to do anything about it (sexual acts between women were assumed to be non-existent). Before that time the state decreed that it was so immoral to engage in homosexual sex that men should be sent to prison for it. This was not a passive law, a long-forgotten relic on the statute books, it was actively enforced. During the 1950s and 1960s a member of the House of Lords with some other men from privileged backgrounds were imprisoned; Alan Turing, a code-breaker from the Second World War credited by many authorities as absolutely critical in cracking Nazi naval secrets, was hounded by the police and committed suicide, having first consented to chemical castration to avoid imprisonment; others lived a secret life in fear of being found out. Established medical opinion was that being gay was abnormal, a diagnosable psychiatric condition that could (albeit with some difficulty) be cured (King and Bartlett, 1999). Those who resisted treatment (including electric shock aversion therapy) were likely to be viewed even by psychiatrists and psychologists (and social workers) through an older perspective: they weren't mad, they were bad; homosexuality was not a sickness, it was a perversion. Gay people were evil.

ACTIVITY 3.1

Consider what the legal difference tells us about the difference between how male sexuality is perceived in contrast to female sexuality. (Perhaps refer to Chapter 2 on gender if you haven't read it already.) Why did the legislators think the law need not include lesbians?

Comment

There is a story that lesbians were not covered in the law because no one dared bring up the subject with Queen Victoria. The truth is that any sexual feelings at all were regarded as unfeminine, so the idea of codifying in law something that didn't really exist did not make sense. The contradiction in all this was the common use of prostitutes by men who could afford them, including doubtless many who sat in Parliament, and the pursuit of actresses and the like who were perceived as enjoying sex. This contradiction was resolved through ideas about social class: women who enjoyed sex were not displaying human sexuality, they were more like animals.

Ten years before the law was changed the *Wolfenden Report* concluded that homosexuality should be legalised (Committee on Homosexual Offences and Prostitution, 1957). The Committee responsible for the report, which carried the approval of the Archbishop of Canterbury, argued that while there was some overlap between morality and law there need not always be. Driving on the left side of the road is compulsory not because it's morally superior but because a morally arbitrary nationwide choice must be made and stuck to. Widespread theft, on the other hand, would lead to social chaos and is also considered morally wrong, so is punishable by law. Adultery is regarded by most people as morally wrong, but it is not covered by criminal law: it is considered an aspect of sexual behaviour – however reprehensible – in which the state has no business interfering. Wolfenden wanted homosexuality to be treated in the same way, and indeed some on the Committee went a step further, arguing that it was not morally wrong either.

It took a decade for the Committee's recommendations to come about, intervening governments believing it was too radical (and therefore too vote-losing) a step to take. It's impossible to know the exact breakdown of views in the general population at the time. Some clearly regarded legalisation as a fatal step towards sanctioning dangerously corrupting immorality, giving space to evil; others saw it as a psychological aberration that needed treatment not punishment; others saw it as no more their business than what their heterosexual neighbours did in bed; still others – we can assume a minority – regarded legalisation as a long overdue recognition of human diversity which would in time allow it to be celebrated. There were contradictions in this. The fourth figure in an old spy scandal, the Cambridge-educated Master of the Queen's Pictures, was known for over a decade to be gay, and it was no secret to the Queen either. The famous composer Benjamin Britten lived openly with his partner Peter Pears for many years, and even in the 1950s and 1960s some performers were 'forgiven' their homosexuality, presumably because they were creative (and no one suggested that the music of Tchaikovsky or the literature of Oscar Wilde was worth less because of the sexual orientation of the artist).

At around the same time the first laws were being passed protecting racial minorities against discrimination and not long afterwards, in 1970, came the Equal Pay Act. This is a striking contrast with the situation for lesbians and gay men. While there were certainly those who argued black people should not exist, at least not in this country, with regular stiffening of immigration control laws and calls for compulsory repatriation (Hiro, 1992) it was becoming recognised, however reluctantly, that treating people differently on the basis of skin colour was indefensible. While Victorian ideas that women should know their (inferior) place had not gone away, no one was saying women should not exist (though implicitly at least there were such assumptions about disabled people). Slightly later than race discrimination laws came the acceptance that it was similarly indefensible to pay a woman less if she was demonstrably doing an identical job as a man for the same employer. The fact that these things were not taken for granted at the time and hence needed legal backing to come about shows how far social attitudes have moved in forty years, yet far from protecting them against discrimination, lesbian and gay people's right to a legitimate existence was barely on the agenda. The best they could hope for was to be allowed privacy, but even this was not to be.

Legal it may have been, but homosexuality was still taboo. Discovery as lesbian, gay or bisexual (hereafter LGB) meant instant dismissal from the armed forces, the civil service and many other jobs, and while there was more latitude for acceptance by individual employers, teachers, medical staff, social workers and many other professionals had no option but to spend their whole lives 'in the closet'. Sections of the media delighted, it seemed, in revealing that some star or public figure was LGB; until a little more than ten years ago the response of 'so what?' was ineffective. Without having to say why, it could simply be assumed that the revelation someone was LGB would make them morally suspect and unfit for public office or social prominence.

AIDS, of course, did not help. An initially deadly and incurable disease more likely to be carried by gay men and intravenous drug users, both stigmatised groups in the first place, would inevitably increase the stigma. The unknown origin of the disease made it easier to label it as a gay plague, and indeed for some to view it as God's punishment for immorality (why lesbians, with a much lower rate of HIV infection than heterosexuals, should be spared this divine curse is not clear). The initial hysteria of the 1980s has diminished somewhat. There is less terror of becoming HIV positive, medical treatments make it no longer a death sentence, and the rate of new infection among heterosexuals is faster than among gay men, but AIDS remains for some people a legitimation of their prejudice against gay men, their homophobia (see www.scottishmediamonitor.com for many years of examples).

Twenty years after legalisation, continuing resistance to changing social attitudes in some powerful quarters was encapsulated in a section of the law referred to in the introductory chapter: section 28 of the 1988 Local Government Act declared: *a local authority shall not intentionally promote homosexuality or publish material with the intention of promoting homosexuality* or *promote the teaching in any maintained school of the acceptability of homosexuality as a pretended family relationship*. In practice this was legally inept, since sex education is the responsibility of school governors not the local authority, and since much of the curriculum is in the hands of teachers, whatever they did would not amount to actions by the local authority. Although no prosecutions ever resulted from this section, it was highly symbolic; it drew a policy line in the sand and took twenty years to repeal. HIV prevention work was specifically excluded from its scope, but there was always concern among HIV prevention agencies and health professionals that it stigmatised gay people and acted as a barrier to useful and frank discussions of issues concerning sexuality in schools.

Clarke's (1998) research into the lives of lesbian physical education teachers demonstrates that the impact of *holding dual identities, i.e. pseudo-heterosexual and lesbian, has the potential to create great dissonance and personal turmoil* (p196). Some women experienced verbal abuse and harassment from pupils and local youths during the time when the implementation of section 28 positioned lesbian and gay sexuality as 'a pretended family relationship'. The women used a range of strategies to disguise or deny their sexuality, including the continued use of married status after divorce or inventing a male partner. One participant in Clarke's research said:

> *Pupils seem to view homosexuality as a deviation from the norm and use the word lessie, or les or gay as an insult not only towards staff but amongst themselves.*

> (Clarke, 1998, p203)

It is important to recognise how quickly things have changed. Since the late 1990s the acceptance of gay people has probably moved at a faster pace than in the previous century, (many of the landmark events are listed in the timeline in Table 3.1). Ward and Carvel (2008) observe that while in 1987 the British Social Attitudes Survey showed that 75 per cent of people thought homosexuality was *always or mostly wrong*, by 2010 this was significantly lower, at 36 per cent. An online survey of over 5,000 people for the Equality and Human Rights Commission (Ellison and Gunstone, 2009) revealed that 83 per cent of heterosexual men and women would be happy or would feel neutral about the prospect of having a manager at work who was openly LGB, 88 per cent felt the same way about having close friends who were openly LGB and 84 per cent felt this about being treated by an openly LGB doctor. Individuals' confidence has grown too:

Seven in ten lesbians (69 per cent) and gay men (70 per cent) felt they could be open about their sexual orientation in the workplace without fear of discrimination or prejudice.

(Ellison and Gunstone, 2009, cited by EHRC, 2009, p19)

Yet it's also important to recognise how much homophobia remains. One in four of the heterosexual respondents to the survey said they would not be happy to vote for an openly LGB candidate for Prime Minister. One in five did not feel that lesbians could be equally good at bringing up children as other women and just over a quarter felt the same about gay men's ability to bring up children as well as other men (Ellison and Gunstone, 2009). Hate crime units report a steady stream of assaults (see below). Bullying related to sexual orientation is at least as widespread in schools as racist bullying and a major source of pain for many young people, one study reporting that 90 per cent of secondary school teachers said that pupils in their schools perceived to be gay are bullied, harassed or called names (Guasp, 2009). Two-thirds of lesbians and gay men report name-calling directed at them. Common culture still generates acceptance of homophobic jokes and to an extent there's a persisting stereotype that true lesbians have cropped hair, tattoos and big boots, while all gay men are effeminate.

ACTIVITY 3.2

Consider (perhaps with reference to Chapter 2 on gender) where these gender stereotypes come from and why they persist. Why is there an idea that there is only one accepted form of masculinity or femininity? Why might it be important that as a social worker you question this?

Comment
There is no escaping the fact that this topic touches many deep-seated ideas. You will see in Chapter 4 on older people that heteronormativity affects them too, often after a lifetime of having to hide who they are. Disabled people are sometimes LGB, as are people from minority ethnic groups.

Table 3.1 Timeline

Before 1800s	Gay male sex was punishable by death. When threat of hanging was removed, the law against homosexuality was strengthened.
1957	Wolfenden Committee recommends legalisation of homosexual acts in private if over 21, but only in England.
1967	Sexual Offences Act legalises homosexuality.
1979	Recommendation made by a Home Office Group that age of consent should be lowered to 18, but nothing happened.
1980	Homosexuality legalised in Scotland (1982 in Northern Ireland).
1983	First openly gay MP (Chris Smith, Labour).
1986	First openly gay character on Eastenders.
1988	Section 28 introduced by Conservative government.

Continued

Table 3.1 *continued*

1990–2	Research on prosecution of gay and bisexual men revealed almost as high as in 1954–5 when homosexuality illegal. Helped pressure police to deprioritise action against victimless gay behaviour and greatly strengthened the case for law reform.
1993	First TV lesbian kiss on *Brookside*.
1994	Under Conservative government, Tory MP Edwina Currie proposed equalisation of the age of consent at 16. Failed, despite large numbers of Labour MPs' support; compromise of 18 was accepted. Male rape for the first time classified as offence.
1997	New Labour government promised to do everything possible to change the law. First openly gay Cabinet minister (Chris Smith).
1998	Age of consent amendment in Crime and Disorder Bill, passed in a free vote in the Commons but thrown out by Lords; government dropped the amendment fearing it would lose the entire Bill. Clause about age of consent reintroduced as the Sexual Offences (Amendment) Bill but defeated again.
1999	Clause about age of consent again reintroduced, with government threatening to enact the Bill regardless of the opinion of the Lords.
1999	Nail bomb planted in popular gay pub in Soho, killing 2, injuring 30.
2000	Lords again throw out amendment but government overrules them using Parliament Act (very rare). Age of consent for homosexual men and women 16 in England, Wales and Scotland, and 17 in Northern Ireland (previously no statutory age of consent for lesbian sex). Ian Paisley ran a *Save Ulster from Sodomy* campaign.
2000	Government tries to repeal section 28, but repeatedly blocked by Lords.
2000	Ban lifted on being openly gay in armed forces.
2001	First openly gay high court judge, also first Metropolitan Police Commander.
2002	First openly gay Conservative MP (Alan Duncan). First uniformed police in London Gay Pride march.
2003	House of Lords agreed to removal of section 28 and rejected amendment to replace it with strict controls on sex education.
2003	Discrimination, harassment and victimisation of gay people in employment made unlawful. Homophobic assault recognised as a hate crime.
2004	Gross indecency and buggery laws repealed (these criminalised consensual sex between gay adults that would be legal for heterosexuals). Males kissing in public previously defined as gross indecency and open to five years' imprisonment.
2004	Gene Robinson, Bishop of New Hampshire, USA, became the first openly gay, non-celibate priest to be ordained as bishop in a major Christian denomination.
2005	Civil partnerships established, giving gay couples equal property and inheritance rights, same pension, immigration and tax status. (Unlike gay partnerships in Belgium, the Netherlands, Spain and Canada, Britain's does not give the legal title of a marriage.)

Some important background

How many gay people are there?

In one way this is irrelevant, just as it makes no difference to an unfairly treated Hindu whether she is one of a hundred or a million. On the other hand, in terms of under-standing the scale of necessary provision, it's useful to know how much of a 'minority' issue this is. There is no official count of LGB people; it's not a census question and it's very rarely monitored on job applications. Hunt and Jensen (2007), citing government actuaries, suggests 6 per cent of the population is LGB, which would mean 156,000 employees in the social and health care sector.

Since being LGB retains some stigma it is inevitable that there will be some under-reporting in anything but an anonymous survey, yet in most of the issues covered in the book monitoring is commonplace. The Census has for decades had no problem asking people their age and sex; since 1991 it asked for ethnicity and in 2001 it asked for religious affiliation too. It's an option on most application forms to state if one is disabled (social class, as discussed in Chapter 1, is not quite the same kind of thing). There will be no question on sexual orientation on the 2011 national Census. However, the Equality and Human Rights Commission argues we have to work towards this kind of monitoring:

> We are aware that the government and other public bodies may lack the confidence to ask for information about sexual orientation. Some people fear that they will be forced to reveal personal information they regard as private; many are concerned that it will fall into the wrong hands. Those are understandable anxieties. That is why our proposals are entirely voluntary – no-one will have to give information they would rather not. But if our society is to be fair to lesbian, gay and bisexual people, it's important to know the facts. Data matters – because injustice that goes unseen goes uncorrected. How can we expect care homes to be sensitive to the needs of older LGB residents, or schools to the needs of the children being brought up by same-sex couples, if they don't even acknowledge they're there? It's important to make the case so that everyone, straight and gay, feels comfortable about volunteering the information, safe in the knowledge that it will be used confidentially and in the interests of making public services work better for everyone.
>
> (EHRC, 2009, p5)

ACTIVITY 3.3

The EHRC goes on to say:

Although it will take time for data collectors and the public to become accustomed to asking and answering sexual orientation questions, this is not a reason for waiting until you get the evidence before you act. Consistency of approach, protecting anonymity and demonstrating how the evidence will be used to good effect are core principles that will reassure the public that their privacy will be protected. *(EHRC, 2009, p16)*

What do you think of this argument? How would you feel about disclosing your sexual orientation? How might you go about asking people that use services about their sexual orientation? What explanation would you give for the need for this information and how it would be used?

Comment

The EHRC is making a distinction between privacy and invisibility, arguing that as long as LGB people are officially invisible, various legitimate needs will not be met. It is still the case, however, especially in areas of low minority ethnic settlement, that ethnic monitoring is done badly. It is often not understood by the (usually white) people doing the monitoring, and it's not always trusted by minorities (some parents insisting their child be listed as white when they quite demonstrably are not).

What causes different sexual orientations?

Common-sense wisdom is very confused about whether homosexuality is the outcome of nature or nurture. This is very relevant to people's prejudices since the belief that homosexuality can be caught, like a disease, affects willingness to be in contact with LGB people and views about adoption and family life, the age of consent and child care provision. As the timeline in Table 3.1 showed, during the early years of this century it took two separate debates and parliamentary decisions to reduce the age of consent for lesbians and gay males. The rationale for a different age was that impressionable young men and women could be made to deviate from the straight path which they would otherwise have taken, so they shouldn't be allowed to make a gay sexual choice until they were three years older than they needed to be to vote or to fight in a war. A similar belief that homosexuality can be caught lies behind some people's anxiety about LGB teachers.

I don't propose to dwell on this debate since I think it's misconceived. Sexual orientation is not the strictly boundaried either/or matter that conventional views suggest; just as gender behaviours are socially constructed (see Chapter 2 on gender) so are sexual orientations. Indeed, all the inequalities examined in this book can be looked at in a similar way: when is someone old or not old? What is the exact borderline between being disabled and not? Is a mixed heritage person black or white? We think the categories have some uses, for example in considering provision, but they should not be prisons.

Confusion with paedophilia

A significant source of hostility towards lesbian and gay people comes from the misinformed idea that they are a predatory threat to minors. This is simply false. A heterosexual male or female may be attracted to younger bodies, older teenagers even, but this does not mean they want to have sex with children. A gay man working in a nursery is no more likely to be sexually attracted to the little boys in his care than his heterosexual female colleagues will want to have sex with the girls. Paedophiles are not necessarily lesbian or gay, and insofar as cases that come to court are an indicator of a wider reality it is clear that children are far more often sexually assaulted by members of the opposite sex (most often men) and indeed members of their own families and adult family friends. 'Stranger danger' is a myth. Detailed figures about this are not kept, but the Home Office tried to unpick the figures covering 2002–3. Their analysis showed there had been 59 abductions by strangers that year and 377 failed attempts by strangers (out of a total of 843 total abductions).

ACTIVITY **3.4**

Is the fear of strangers and indeed some professionals a reflection of the wish that all families are safe places? What are the implications of this for social workers? What does this do to girls and boys who experience abuse within their families or social networks that should be safe environments?

Comment

In some ways the particular fear of men working with young children is about the disruption of gender roles that they represent. If looking after small children is basically women's work, for which nature has suited them, then a man who does this can't be a real man: to square the circle he has to be perceived as gay.

Homophobia and its consequences

Being LGB is not in itself a cause of depression or distress. Jews do not spend their lives wishing they were Christian, nor Caribbean people wishing they were Indian, nor indeed do all disabled people wish away their disability. We might ask how many straight people wish they were gay? The problems of being part of a minority group spring largely from others' reaction to you, from the process of othering. Thus the organisation *Schools Out* reports thousands of cases of unhappy teenagers agonising about their sexual identity (Warwick, et al., 2004) terrified of being thought gay and struggling to be 'normal'. Becoming perceived as gay can make their lives a misery, but it's the perception that makes this happen, not the orientation itself. *Nearly four in ten lesbians and gay men reported that they had been bullied, felt frightened and had suffered from low self-esteem* (Ellison and Gunstone, 2009, cited by EHRC, 2009, p9).

Hate crime

This is the most extreme manifestation of hostility towards LGB people, and several police forces have established hate crime units, originally targeted at racist crime but now frequently extended to cover homophobic crime as well (extreme right-wing literature suggests that the same neo-Nazi ideas inform them both).

The evidence of the extent of hate crime is alarming and is sometimes in stark contrast to some of the more positive signs of progress reported earlier. *Around one in five gay men ... reported they had been physically assaulted* (EHRC, 2009, p30) and in a study for Stonewall, Dick (2008) found that one in eight lesbian and gay men and one in 20 bisexuals had experienced a hate crime or incident in the previous year. This makes ordinary everyday life problematic, with only around a quarter of lesbians and gay men feeling able to be open about their sexual orientation, holding hands walking down the street in their local neighbourhood (Ellison and Gunstone, 2009). The same study found that *55 per cent of gay men, 51 per cent of lesbians and 21 per cent of bisexual women and men said they would not live in certain places in Britain because of their sexual orientation* (Ellison and Gunstone, 2009, cited by EHRC, p30) with only around half of lesbians and gay men believing they could be open about their sexual orientation in their local police station without fear of prejudice and discrimination.

Workplace homophobia

Depending on your views of these occupations you may or may not be surprised to learn that the EHRC reports *perceptions and experiences of homophobia, particularly in the police service and armed forces, teaching and manual trades, as reasons for avoiding particular professions for some LGB people* (EHRC, 2009, p20), while on the other hand Stonewall rates very highly the monitoring on grounds of sexual orientation at Goldman Sachs, Barclays, LloydsTSB and IBM (EHRC, 2009). In universities, about a third of LGB staff experience negative treatment from colleagues and about a fifth from students (Hunt and Jensen, 2007).

Much as LGB schoolchildren live in fear, so do adults in some workplaces. The partner of one gay man said:

> *He basically spends half his waking day pretending to be someone he's not, and he daren't raise the issue of the homophobic culture with his manager for fear of reprisal. I can't help but wonder how many other LGB people are succeeding in their jobs, but at the price of hiding their sexuality.*
>
> (EHRC, 2009, p20)

What of social care and health? Stonewall was commissioned in 2007 to investigate the experiences of gay people working within these fields. Their study doesn't claim to be representative but *participants are drawn from a range of locations and work in a variety of sectors. Their experiences suggest that deep-rooted discriminatory practices do occur across the sector, notwithstanding examples of good practice in many places* (Hunt, et al., 2007, p3).

Interviewees found there were rather more homophobic comments if they had disclosed their own sexuality. These included referring to lesbian clients as disgusting and graffiti on LGB staff's lockers. Several commented on the necessity of constantly lying or covering up about their home lives, remembering to refer to their partners with the right pronoun, and inventing false names. Some who were 'out' spoke of persistent attempts by religious colleagues to convince them of the sinfulness of their ways (including a manager who said she was a *Christian first, an NHS manager second* (Hunt, et al., 2007, p18). One social work student recounted being perceived as militant and extreme simply because she declared her sexual orientation, and when suggesting that such a perception was heterosexist her supervisor responded that she *wasn't going to apologise for being heterosexual and that she didn't have time to be PC about everything* (Hunt, et al., 2007, p13). Another said:

> *I had just started work as a project worker at a hostel for homeless teens. Within half an hour of arriving and meeting my colleagues, I was asked by one of them if I was gay [...] She then proceeded to tell me that I should take lengths to disguise my sexuality because a previous member of staff had had to quit because of the homophobic abuse he was receiving from service users.*
>
> (Ibid., p16)

As the authors observed, it is surprising that the previous incident had not spurred on the employer to support LGB staff better; not only was their response inadequate, it was unlawful.

Most participants in the survey were aware that their employer had mechanisms for reporting and dealing with discrimination, but *many were unsure that anti-gay discrimination would be taken seriously enough for a complaint to be processed and the perpetrator to be disciplined* (ibid., p23), partly because they weren't confident their employers understood what homophobia was.

Consider whether you have a homophobic culture in your workplace (or campus). Have you:

- *heard homophobic language;*

- *noticed any covert or explicit exclusion of lesbian, gay and bisexual colleagues, either professionally or socially;*

- *witnessed explicit derision of lesbian, gay and bisexual people;*

- *witnessed managers ignoring or contributing towards homophobic comments and incidents;*

- *seen any sign of your employer trying to prevent homophobia (e.g. in policies or training)?*

Comment

The participants in the Stonewall survey were very clear about what needed to happen to prevent discrimination. They wanted:

- better training for colleagues;

- more robust and accessible policies;

- an increase in visibility of LGB role models;

- confidence that they would not be victimised if they made a complaint;

- managers who understand the law and the duties they have to protect staff;

- networks to reduce local and national isolation.

Implications for social workers

There's a reason I have dwelt here on workplace homophobia. It is an index of general social attitudes if social work staff experience homophobia from comments, and it has real implications for service users. If staff are not always confident of receiving fair and unprejudiced treatment, how might clients feel?

> *I want to be able to be gay in my last days. I don't want to have to hide again and I particularly don't want to have to hide because the home help is coming round ...*

> (Pugh, 2008, cited in EHRC, p11)

Age Concern has produced a guide containing some myths about lesbians and gay men (Smith and Clavert, 2001) that have implications for other areas of social work:

- *There aren't any round here* This is based on the belief that lesbians and gay men are easily identified by their appearance and behaviour, thus recycling stereotypes pertaining to masculine lesbians and effeminate gay men.

- *They can look after their own* A similar rationale has been used not to provide services for black and minority ethnic people. Lesbians and gay men have indeed developed some services to meet social care and health needs (Terence Higgins Trust, National Gay Funeral Helpline) and political campaigning organisations (Outrage!, Stonewall), but why do you think this is?

- *We're open to everyone anyway* Several studies noted in this chapter demonstrate this is not the case, but here is one more: some lesbians and gay men living in care homes *may feel compelled to veil their sexuality* (Ward, et al., 2005, p53).

- *No one's ever asked for specific services for lesbian and gay men, so obviously there is no need* Lesbians and gay men are not a homogenous group and do not have one collective voice. It's worth noting how contradictory myths nevertheless reinforce each other – compare this to the second myth and the next one.

- *We already have lesbian and gay clients – they just don't flaunt it* A common critique of lesbian and gay men has been the alleged flaunting of their sexual orientation, conflating a social identity solely with sexual practices. It's interesting to reword this myth in terms of ethnicity or age.

- *They keep themselves to themselves* (except, presumably, for those who flaunt it). Given the uncertainty and anxiety revealed in various studies about declaring one's sexual orientation, some reticence is not surprising. As Butler (1993) observes, the assumption of 'compulsory heterosexuality' (heteronormativity) means, for instance, that lesbian and gay male carers invariably have to come out to multiple professionals.

(Adapted from Smith and Clavert, 2001, pp8–12)

ACTIVITY **3.6**

Consider the following two comments from researchers:

There is little point ... in a social worker making a referral for a lesbian or a gay man to attend a day centre, or residential respite unit, as a means of alleviating loneliness, when they cannot openly discuss their lives ... The majority of residents are unlikely to have a liberal attitude towards fellow residents who are lesbian or gay, having grown up in less tolerant times.

(Concannon, 2007, p406)

There is a well argued view that lesbians and gay men may find the process of ageing and caring less destabilising than heterosexual counterparts due to the resilience that they have developed throughout their lives in dealing with homophobia, marginalisation and a stigmatised identity. In addition the roles are not gendered as often occurs in heterosexual couples, so the capacity to deal with a range of daily living tasks such as domestic work and financial matters are skills that both partners have, whereas older heterosexual women may have difficulty managing financial matters, while their husbands are unable to care for themselves domestically. This creates particular difficulties if one partner is unable to do these tasks due to ill health. Older lesbians and gay men may not have children and will therefore have invested time in developing social networks to reduce isolation. This again is a strength, as they have support as they age.

(Brown Cosis, 1998)

How do these relate to the myths listed in the previous section?

Comment

The second quotation reminds us that while this book dwells a lot on the negative consequences of not recognising diversity, we need to remember a point made in the opening
chapter and stated a good deal in Chapter 5 about disability: being different is not
inherently a curse; a diverse society is not to be regarded as burdensome or regrettable. It
just is – it's the nature of human beings.

CASE STUDY

*St Joseph's is a day centre catering mostly for young adults with learning disabilities. It
has always had strong links with the Catholic Church which provides its premises. The
manager has encouraged the development of open discussion about sex, a sensitive issue
with several families.*

*George was appointed two years ago. He is currently applying for a promotion at the
centre and has had indications that he has a good chance of success. It is a largely white
neighbourhood and George is the only black member of staff. He has taken the lead role
in some of the sex education work going on at the centre.*

*An influential benefactor and local business leader, who has always been very active in
fundraising, has told the manager that he believes George is gay. He is unhappy about
George being involved in sex education work and about his own son being cared for by
him, and he wants the manager to talk to George.*

*George often confides in Jim, a colleague. Jim tells him the manager is going to ask him
to confirm whether or not he is gay. George says he will refuse to answer such a question
as it is irrelevant to his job. He asks Jim if he can count on his support.*

- *Should the manager say anything to George, and if so, what?*

- *Should the manager say anything to the benefactor/fundraiser. If so, what?*

- *What would you do or offer to do as a colleague of George?*

- *What would you do if you were George?*

C H A P T E R   S U M M A R Y

This chapter shows the pace of positive change with regard to sexual orientation at the same time as continuing vari-
ation in social attitudes. Complete acceptance coexists with deep-seated revulsion, sometimes legitimated by fears of
corrupting the young and sometimes by religious principle. It has also covered the network of interwoven assumptions
that maintain heteronormativity.

WEBSITES

Stonewall's guide *What's it got to do with you?* (2009) helps address concerns on monitoring sexual
orientation. (Downloadable at **www.stonewall.org.uk/what_we_do/2583.asp**)

www.Coastkid.org

The anti-bullying website contains fictionalised characters involved in bullying and being bullied. Two
of them have their own issues around sexual orientation.

Chapter 4
Older people

Gill Constable

Introduction

This chapter will develop our understanding of social work practice with older people, although old age alone is not a rationale for social work engagement. There are other issues such as mental health needs, learning difficulties or sensory and physical impairments. We will start by reflecting on our understanding of ageing and place this in the context of culture, theory and social policy. The aim will be to develop practice that is reflective, critical and anti-oppressive towards older people.

What is old age?

The process of growing older is important for all of us as it affects our own lives, families and friends. At what age are we old? Tanner and Harris (2008) give three approaches that are used to define age: chronological age, the process of physical ageing and health needs as they relate to behaviour and abilities.

The most common definition used in health and social care services is chronological age. People are allocated to particular services on the basis of both need and age. For example, mental health services are arranged in discrete age cohorts: child and adolescence, working age adults and older people. Retirement from work for the majority of people occurs in their sixties, and occupational and state pensions then become available to them. How age is defined in the United Kingdom is set down in terms of organisational factors that relate to the needs of an effective and efficient infrastructure. Lives are structured by chronological age without consideration of other factors.

The meanings given to different chronological ages can be seen as socially constructed. Dalrymple and Burke (2006) explain that social construction as a theory has developed from postmodernism, which challenges universal theories and absolute truths. Due to societal complexity and political and cultural diversity, old age does not have a universal definition. It is dependent on the cultural and social context of the person and their own understanding of old age.

Lawrence and Simpson (2009, p78) state that the life expectancy in the United Kingdom is 81 years for women and 77 years for men, in contrast to sub-Saharan Africa where the average age on death is the early 40s. ... *old age is obviously viewed differently and tends to be thought of as being relatively earlier than in countries with a higher life expectancy* (p78). This statistic is truly shocking and demonstrates the scale of global inequality. Being old in sub-Saharan Africa will not be understood in the same way as being old in Britain.

Age discrimination

Age discrimination can be defined as discriminatory attitudes, behaviour and inequalities in terms of entitlements, choices and services towards people based on age. It can affect younger people as well older people. Thompson (2001, p88) argues that:

Age is a social division; it is a dimension of the social structure on the basis of which power, privilege and opportunities tend to be allocated. Age is not just a simple matter of biological maturation – it is a highly significant social indicator.

Tanner and Harris (2008) identify three causes of age discrimination.

1. *Economic* Within capitalism people are valued as workers – if people are not in paid employment they are perceived as not contributing.

2. *Cultural* Older people are seen as taking up health and social care resources, as a burden, because of ageing populations in the western world. These sentiments are expressed by terms such as *an ageing world* or *global greying* (Graham, 2007, p144).

3. *Interpersonal* Older people may be perceived as the 'other', due to fears about ageing and death.

Age discrimination is now unlawful in employment, education and training under the Employment Equality (Age) Regulations 2006. This enables people to work until they are 65 years old. Tanner and Harris (2008) view this as being less about social justice and more a response to an increasingly ageing population and government need to reduce spending on pensions, benefits and public services.

Ageism

Age discrimination means that people are denied the rights that other citizens have on the basis of age. By contrast, ageism identifies oppressive attitudes, values and beliefs that are culturally reinforced and impact negatively on the well-being of older people.

Tanner and Harris (2008, p13) state:

> *Cross-cultural and historical perspectives are helpful in reinforcing our understanding of the ageist social construction of old age as the dominant discourse in western societies. Unfortunately, in that discourse, old age is socially constructed as 'problem'. This social construction of old age confers a loss of status and a devalued identity on older people.*

The concept of old age is often disparaged and not accorded respect, in contrast to many other societies where older people are seen as resources of experience, knowledge and expertise. Thompson (2001, p90) sets out a series of assumptions that are made about older people, which encapsulate ageism.

- *Old equals useless* This links with economic factors that perpetuate age discrimination. Older people are seen as unproductive. This assumption fails to acknowledge the contribution that older people make within their families and the community, such as being grandparents, carers, volunteers, consumers and so on.

- *Old equals childlike* This can result in older people being infantilised and their experience, knowledge and skills not being recognised, valued or fully utilised.

- *Old equals ill* Health needs are put down to old age, and therefore health complaints are not taken seriously and treatment not provided.

- *Old equals not ill* This is a common belief, resulting in ailments being put down to old age and therefore not worth treating. For example, only one third of people with dementia obtain a diagnosis and are provided with appropriate treatment. This results in people not being able to make choices or plans for their future.

- *Old equals lonely* This ignores older people's networks and contacts, as well as assuming that older people do not make new friends. Loneliness is not just experienced by some older people; it can affect many people at different stages of life, including the young.

- *Old equals unintelligent* Older people can be seen as slower in their comprehension and this leads to a patronising approach towards them, with assumptions being made that all older people are confused and unreliable when providing information. This concept gets played out in common comments such as a social work manager saying in a meeting, 'I am just having a grey moment' as an explanation for forgetting a piece of information.

- *Old equals inhuman* Placing older people in a separate category through the use of terms such as 'the elderly', 'elderly mental infirm', 'geriatrics', or coastal areas with significant populations of older people known as 'Costa Del Geriatrica' and so on.

- *Old equals poor* A significant number of older people do live in poverty but this is not a factor for everyone. There are five and a half million people of retirement age living abroad, many of whom have migrated with amassed wealth and occupational pensions (Lawrence and Simpson, 2009, p79). An assumption of poverty can prevent older people accessing choices and options.

- *Old equals asexual* Making an assumption that older people have no interest in sex any more, and if they ever did it was in heterosexual sex. Sexuality is part of being human and to deny this in older people is to treat them as less than human, and additionally being lesbian, gay or bisexual pertains to a sense of identity and community (Commission for Social Care Inspection, 2008).

Denzin (1989, p73) states that *no self or personal experience story is ever an individual production.* Hence, older people can internalise feelings of ageism and experience a loss of self-esteem and this will impact on their sense of identity. In other words, the assumptions that Thompson (2001) has articulated can become beliefs held by older people themselves. Beliefs are not necessarily based on any factual evidence; they are simply what we choose to tell ourselves. If these beliefs are partly confirmed by how we are treated by others they can become self-narratives.

ACTIVITY 4.1

Consider this in relation to these four verses taken from 'Provide, Provide', a poem written by Robert Frost in 1936 (in Ferguson, et al., 2005, p1241). What is your response to these verses? Summarise what the poet is saying about women and ageing.

The witch that came (the withered hag)
To wash the step with pail and rag,
Was once the beauty Abishag,*

The picture pride of Hollywood.
Too many fall from the great and good
For you to doubt the likelihood.

Continued

ACTIVITY *4.1* *continued*

Die early and avoid the fate.
Or if predestined to die late,
Make up your mind to die in state.

No memory of having starred
Atones for later disregard,
Or keeps the end from being hard.

(*Abishag was a young woman brought to King David in the Bible (1 Kings 1: 2–4) in his old age with the intention of meeting his physical and sexual needs.*)

Comment

The poem is about the transient nature of beauty, within the context of the Hollywood film industry. It uses harsh and discriminatory language: *the witch that came* (the withered hag). If you reflect on celebrity culture with its focus on young people, and then think about how often you see middle-aged or older people especially women – in the media, how frequently are the joys and achievements of old age celebrated? Frost's hectoring poem seems as apt today as when it was written in 1936.

RESEARCH SUMMARY

The highest incidence of suicide occurs with people aged over 75 years. Depression disproportionately impacts on older people, and it is estimated that 10% of people aged over 65 years experience depression that is sufficiently persistent, and severe to require professional intervention. There are ten million people of retirement age, which is over 20% of Britain's population. Therefore at any one time up to one million older people may be experiencing depression.

(Golightley, 2008, pp100–1)

It is important as a social worker that you are aware of the above research. Do not assume that depression is a normal part of old age. It is just as concerning as depression in younger people and can be treated effectively once recognised.

One approach that promotes well-being is reminiscence. It can enhance self-esteem, as knowledge is transferred to the person listening and it provides the opportunity to develop a sense of self through memories. Encouraging people to think about their strengths is more hopeful and purposeful than dwelling on difficulties (Schweitzer and Bruce, 2008). We will now consider theories of ageing and critically evaluate them in relation to their impact on the development and delivery of services to older people.

Theories of ageing

By exploring theories of ageing we will better understand the experience of becoming older, and how these different theoretical perspectives influence and underpin the configuration of services. The following definition from Oko (2008, p6) will be used:

... a theory can be described as representing a set of related ideas and assumptions that are drawn upon to help explain a particular phenomenon. A theory represents an explanatory framework which attempts to help us make sense of the phenomenon in question ... These explanations provide us with the opportunity to hypothesise, or make a judgement about what we think is going on.

Tanner and Harris (2008, p28) have developed the approach in Table 4.1 to evaluate and question theoretical perspectives pertaining to ageing which are worth considering prior to looking at the theories.

Table 4.1 Critical questions to evaluate theories of ageing

	Theoretical approach	Evaluative questions
1.	Consensual versus conflictual view of society	Does the theory assume that society is working positively for people and maintaining the status quo appropriately, or does it see society controlling policy and resources so some groups gain at the expense of others?
2.	Deficit versus heroic models of ageing	Does the theory see old age as a process of decline in contrast to old age being full of activity?
3.	Social determinism versus individual agency and resistance	Does the theory view the lives of older people as controlled by political, social and economic factors over which they have no control, as opposed to older people shaping their lives through their actions?
4.	Homogeneity versus diversity	Are all older people assumed to be similar, or are older people seen as diverse due to their biographies, culture, gender, sexuality, ethnic origin and class?
5.	Stasis versus change and fluidity	Are society and older people seen as static, in contrast to engaging in change and personal development?

Eight theories about ageing

Biological theories (deficit versus heroic)
Ageing is seen as a biological and physiological process that ends in physical decline and death. It does not take account of individual differences through societal, cultural and environmental factors. Medical problems tend to be blamed on ageing and may not be fully investigated. It can make people feel anxious and fearful about old age. It is a deficit rather than heroic view of ageing.

Erikson's life cycle (homogeneity versus diversity)
This theory was developed by Erikson (1977) and views life as comprising eight stages. A successful transition process has to be negotiated from one stage to the next to achieve a sense of well-being. The theory assumes that life is a clearly defined trajectory with events such as education and being a parent occurring at the same time for everyone. It is ethnocentric, heterosexist and assumes homogeneity rather than diversity in the experience of ageing, since older people can access university, start new activities, begin new relationships and so on.

Disengagement theory (deficit versus heroic)
Cummings and Henry (1961) developed this theory. It envisages older people positively handing over responsibilities to young people and withdrawing from life. Old age is seen

as a time of stagnation and decline. It assumes that all older people wish to become socially inactive. Like the biological theory, it is a deficit understanding of ageing.

Activity theory (deficit versus heroic)

Activity is seen as significant for older people including those with cognitive impairments such as dementia, though older people should be able to choose the activities that they engage in rather than this being assumed for them. For example, many older people do not enjoy bingo, yet this is often an activity that is provided in day centres and care homes. Overall this theory is heroic in its evaluation of ageing, as it stresses purposefulness and vitality.

Continuity theory (social determinism versus individual agency and resistance)

This theory assumes that older people manage change by retaining the ideas, skills and preferred activities within their usual environment. The theory focuses on the individual and does not take account of their social context over which they may have limited or no control. An example would be an older person living in a first-floor housing complex without a lift becoming housebound as they can no longer use the stairs. They may wish to continue to live in their flat, but due to factors out of their control their quality of life has been adversely affected.

Structured dependency (social determinism versus individual agency and resistance)

A theory of ageing that emphasises that the experience of being older is determined by social and health care policies, retirement plans and pensions that reduce many people to poverty in old age. Care services that are provided are difficult to access and socially exclude older people from the rest of the community through segregated provision based on age. The theory does not recognise that older people do challenge oppressive social and health policies. Many people save for their retirement. In addition people may assess the quality of their lives positively even if their financial circumstances are problematic.

Identity management theory (stasis versus change and fluidity)

This is a postmodern theory that sees identity as fluid over the course of a lifetime, and that people make choices that determine how they live their lives. It does not take account of structural factors that limit choice. Issues of diversity and individual agency are prominent.

Life course theory (homogeneity versus diversity)

This theory emphasises that ageing should be understood within the context of the life that has been lived. It adopts a biographical approach that includes the wider social, economic and political factors that have in part influenced the person's life choices.

Comment on the theories

A number of the theories have elements that can be supportive and positive in working with older people. Often a range of theoretical perspectives taking a specific component rather than the whole theory can be useful to inform practice. Tanner and Harris (2008) conclude their overview of theories by emphasising the need for social workers to engage with older people and discover how *they* theorise their own ageing.

We will now explore a case study to examine how theoretical perspectives impact on the design and delivery of services for older people. Social workers have a key role in assessing and monitoring the quality of services provided to older people.

CASE STUDY

Hannah was in the first week of her social work placement in an Adults' Services Team. As part of her induction her practice assessor had asked her to visit Autumn Time Home. *Prior to visiting Hannah accessed the inspection report for the home on the Care Quality Commission's website to gain some background information about the home. She decided to ask to spend half a day in the home. Hannah asked to be shown around and then requested to sit with the residents in the communal lounge. These are Hannah's notes from her visit:*

Autumn Time Home

When I arrived at the home I noticed that it was well maintained with beautiful hanging baskets and a well tended garden. I did not get a response when I rang the bell. A member of staff arrived for her shift and she let me in saying that it was really busy inside to explain why no one answered the door.

I was left in the hall for a while waiting for the deputy manager who finally appeared. He looked really harassed. I was shown around. The overall atmosphere was noisy with staff rushing around, and bells from people's rooms ringing. I noticed a smell of urine several times. In the lounge there were about fifteen people seated all against the walls. There was very little happening. Staff popped in and out, but no real interaction taking place between the residents or with the staff. The contrast between the staff's activity and the residents' passivity was very marked.

The deputy manager was happy for me to sit in the lounge, but he expressed some surprise, as he explained most of the residents were confused, so it would be difficult to have a conversation with anyone. I explained that I had brought some photographs and objects that I thought may be of interest. I was aware that a number of the residents were Caribbean so I had downloaded photographs of the *Windrush*. The *Empire Windrush* was the first passenger ship to bring postwar immigrants from Jamaica to the UK in 1948. London Transport Buses, Jamaica, St Lucia and so on. It was a series of pictures that I thought I could talk to people about. I brought some household objects along too: a scrubbing board, whistling kettle, cranking handle, and a shaving brush, as well as some Caribbean music.

I had a really enjoyable afternoon with the residents. The pictures and objects aroused a lot of interest. Some of the residents sang songs, and we even had a little dance. A couple of the staff joined us and the afternoon ended with a cup of tea. The deputy manager asked me if I could visit again. He said he was really keen to develop a person-centred approach in the home, as he knew it was very task-orientated. I agreed to go back again and we talked about my setting up a reminiscence group with some of the residents.

---

1. *What theories of ageing do you think were being implemented in* Autumn Time Home?

2. *What theoretical perspectives was Hannah implementing?*

3. *Is group work a competency in the National Occupational Standards for Social Work?*

4. *What is person-centred practice in contrast to task-centred practice?*

Comment

From Hannah's description it sounds as if the home's care practice is informed by disengagement theory. While the name of the home is suggestive of Erikson's life cycle theory. Hannah clearly has other ideas. She has carefully prepared for her visit. She has undertaken some research by reading the inspection report which has enabled her to learn about the ethnic origins and needs of the residents, as well as the quality of care provided. She is using activity theory but is providing the residents with the choice as to whether they wish to join in, and life course theory.

Competence in group work is a National Occupational Standard: Key Role 2: Unit 8 *Work with groups to promote individual growth, development and independence.* This must be met on social work practice placements.

Person-centred practice can be defined as meeting people's individual needs through a knowledge and understanding of the person's biography and their preferences in how they wish to live their life. This includes things such as preferred clothing, food, hobbies, music and so on. Task-orientated practice means that care is delivered through undertaking a range of practical tasks in a similar manner to everyone with no account of their needs and wishes. Examples are not giving residents any choice about when they get up in the morning or what they do during the day, allowing no meal choices and so on.

Social policy and the ageing process

The development of social policy has moved from the social exclusion of older people with physical, sensory or mental health needs within institutions to care in the community, which was implemented through the National Health Service (NHS) and Community Care Act 1990. Care in the Community as a policy sought to enable adults with health and social care needs be supported with care services in their own homes rather than being admitted to a long-stay hospital, nursing or residential care provision.

Table 4.2 is an adaptation of Payne's (1995, p33) history of social policy. Personalisation is now being implemented where older people with health and social care needs are provided with funding for them to choose the services they want rather than services being arranged for them.

Table 4.2 Payne's history of social policy

Historical and developmental phase	Social care legislation and policy
Institutional phase: end of nineteenth century	Poor Law 1834 and the establishment of workhouses and hospital 'asylums' for people with mental health needs, learning difficulties, physical and sensory disabilities for children and adults.
Commitment phase: first part of the twentieth century	The development of the welfare state through the Beveridge Report 1942, and the eradication of the 'five giant evils' (disease, idleness, ignorance, squalor and want) through the provision of the NHS, full employment, state education, public housing and National Insurance and Assistance schemes to reduce poverty (Alcock, 2003, p6). Dominant model of care continued to be institutions for adults.
Community collective phase: 1960s/1970s	Seebohm Report 1968 led to the merging of Children's Departments with Welfare and Health Departments, through the creation of Social Services Departments. Concept of services delivered to children and adults through generic social workers. Continued dependence on institutional forms of long-term care for adults in need.
Individualised phase: 1980s onwards	NHS and Community Care Act 1990 focused on supporting adults within their homes. *Putting People First* (Department of Health, 2008b) has enabled services to become personalised as people choose the services they need.

CASE STUDY

We will now consider how theories of ageing and social policy impact on social work practice. Read the following case study and answer the questions at the end.

Connor is a social work student on placement in a day centre for older people managed by a voluntary sector organisation. The centre has some activities that enable people to drop in without a referral from a health or social care professional. One of the services that the centre offers is information, advice and support to informal carers, that is family and friends who are unpaid carers of people with dementia.

Connor was supporting Sylvia, a member of staff who was running the group. During an information session about dementia one of the carers became visibly very upset and got up to leave. Connor followed the man (Bill) out and invited him into a quiet room for a discussion. Below is an extract from Connor's reflective journal.

Bill (79 years) and Patrick (82 years)

It was the first time that Bill had attended the Carers' Group. He looked very frail and anxious. His breathing was quite laboured and he used a walking stick. I felt overwhelmed by his distress. He put his head in his hands and wept, and he was having real trouble catching his breath. I tried to reassure him. He told me he hadn't understood that dementia is a degenerative illness and that his friend, Patrick, who has just started attending the centre, wouldn't get better.

I asked him what he had been told by the doctor. Bill told me he was never included in any discussions with health staff, although he took Patrick to appointments. He thought that the medication that he had been given would make him better. Bill said that Patrick's confusion was getting worse, and at times he got very frustrated and angry. I had this sense that this was a very significant relationship. I made the decision to ask if Patrick was

Continued

his partner. He confirmed that he was, and told me no one had asked before. Bill spent a lot of time with Patrick caring for him, although they don't live together.

Bill told me that he felt quite hopeless and desperate about things. Their life together before Patrick's illness had been very happy, and he found the changes in Patrick's behaviour difficult to manage. For example, Patrick wanted to go to church, which he hadn't done since he was a young man. Bill said that Patrick's family live in Glasgow and now comprised just two great nephews, and there was no contact. There had been a problematic relationship with his sister and their mother, prior to her death, due to his sexual orientation. Bill explained that they had friends, but many of them were getting older, and the more difficult Patrick's behaviour became the less contact they had. Bill told me he didn't want Patrick to be taken away, and that they could cope. He became very agitated by this thought.

I felt so concerned about Bill that I suggested that I visited him and Patrick at home to see what we could do to help. He was really grateful, and became quite calm. He said he felt better and that he was OK to take Patrick home from the centre. He checked with me before he left that I would not get the 'welfare' to take Patrick away.

1. *Imagine that you are Connor. How might you prepare for your home visit to Bill and Patrick?*

2. *What do you think has prompted Bill's anxiety that Patrick might be 'taken away'?*

3. *What might be the reasons that Bill's role as a carer was not recognised by health staff?*

Comment

In preparation for the visit to Bill and Patrick, Connor checked the file held on Patrick at the centre. He noted that Patrick had referred himself having seen a poster in the doctor's surgery about the service, and there was no involvement from Adults' Services. The details about Patrick were very limited and only amounted to his name, address, age, ethnic origin which was Irish/Scottish, and that he was a Roman Catholic (lapsed). The referral form asked questions about marital status but did not give any prompt for partners or civil partners. It was recorded that he was unmarried and lived alone.

Being 'research minded', Connor accessed the local authority's website and contacted the National Lesbian, Gay, Bisexual and Transgendered Switchboard to obtain advice and information about resources (he preserved confidentiality by not naming Bill or Patrick). Connor approached his preparatory work with an understanding that: ... *human identity is narrational, lives being composed of the narratives by which time is experienced* (Erben, 1998, p11). During much of Bill's and Patrick's lifetime male homosexuality was illegal, and was only partially decriminalised for men by the Sexual Offences Act 1967, although the Merchant Navy and Armed Forces were excluded. It was not until the Sexual Offences Act 2000 that the age of consent was equalised between gay men and heterosexuals. Discrimination on the basis of sexual orientation only became unlawful in 2007 through the Equality Act (Sexual Orientation) Regulations and applies primarily to the provision of goods and services. The requirements do not include religious organisations. Bill and Patrick are likely to have experienced multiple oppressions (Thompson, 2001, p103) on the basis of their age, sexuality and health needs and Bill's concern that the 'welfare' would remove Patrick was founded on his memories of older people with mental health needs being placed on geriatric wards in a psychiatric hospital. Connor's research enabled him to develop an understanding of the social context of their lives and in the event Bill and Patrick were keen for Connor to advocate and guide them through the health and social care system. Together the following was achieved:

- Patrick wanted Bill to be included in all his consultations with his GP and old age psychiatrist. Connor supported them to ensure this happened.

- With Patrick and Bill's agreement, Connor referred them to Adults' Services. Connor supported them in ensuring that assessments were completed under the NHS and Community Care Act 1990 and Carers (Recognition and Services) Act 2000. Patrick and Bill were able to recruit their own personal assistants to support Patrick as the dementia progressed, and for Bill to receive some respite from caring.

- Connor told Patrick and Bill about the Metropolitan Community Church which ministers to lesbians, gay men, bisexual and transgendered people. The church was very affirmative and supportive. Patrick and Bill attended services and joined the Singing Group, and became part of the church community. This had a very significant impact on Patrick, and appeared to provide him with emotional comfort.

- Connor offered to assist the manager of the day centre in auditing the service using the checklist in *Putting people first: equality and diversity matters* (Commission for Social Care Inspection, 2008, p38) to ensure that the service promoted and welcomed diversity and equality in all its aspects. Connor was asked by the manager to be part of the planning team for a staff workshop on sexual orientation and inclusive practice.

Connor learnt a great deal from his involvement with Bill and Patrick, and in particular the importance of developing an understanding of people's life history and the social and cultural context in which they have lived their lives.

C H A P T E R   S U M M A R Y

This chapter has considered the experience of ageing and the impact of discrimination and ageism on older people. It has evaluated theories of ageing and considered how they are implemented in the delivery of care services. The impact of multiple oppressions has been explored. The importance of social workers being 'research minded', reflective and curious about older people's biographies and the social context of their lives has been given particular prominence.

FURTHER READING

Tanner, D and Harris, J (2008) *Working with older people*. Abingdon: Routledge.

This is a comprehensive book, and includes theory, practice and the skills required to work effectively with older people.

Thompson, N (2006) *Anti-discriminatory practice*. 4th edition. Basingstoke: Palgrave.

This book tackles the range of oppressions experienced by people. Its style is concise and very accessible; it deals with complex issues very effectively.

Chapter 5
Celebrating disability

Colin Goble

Introduction

In this chapter I am going to advocate the idea that we should celebrate human diversity. There's nothing particularly controversial about that, you might think. We are quite used to this idea when it comes to thinking about areas like culture, ethnicity, gender and sexual orientation. And of course recognising and valuing diversity are regarded as basic virtues and values in social work and social care, linked to concepts such as anti-oppressive and anti-discriminatory practice (Banks, 2006). However, I am going to take the idea of celebrating diversity somewhat further than we are perhaps used to, applying it to a group of people that we are not used to thinking about in such a positive way – that most diverse of all social groups that fall under the broad category of disabled people.

Recent years have seen some significant advances in recognising that disability should be treated as an issue of rights and discrimination rather than as a purely biomedical phenomenon. This idea is enshrined, for example, in the Disability Discrimination Act 1995, and further enhanced in subsequent legislation, such as the Human Rights Act 1998 and the Mental Capacity Act 2007. A rights-based approach to disability is also dominant in other areas of government policy, such as the current 'transformation agenda' in social care which draws heavily and explicitly on the social model of disability (e.g. Commission for Social Care Inspection (CSCI), 2009).

The idea that we might go beyond challenging discrimination against disabled people and that disability might be something that can actually be celebrated is still relatively new and controversial, however. It is an idea that draws on radical, so-called 'postmodern', theoretical perspectives developed in recent decades in the social sciences (e.g. Leonard, 1997; Sampson, 1993), and the politics of identity, which has roots in feminist thought but has more recently been applied in the field of disability studies (e.g. Corker, 1996; Corker and Shakespeare, 2002). These developments have led to the emergence of what has been called the affirmative model of disability that seeks not to replace the social model but to extend the argument on which it is based a stage further. The argument is that, if not for all, then for many disabled people, life is not tragic, full of suffering and woe, but enjoyable, with a significant and sometimes enhanced element of pleasure, creativity and fulfilment, and that the experience of impairment should not be assumed always to represent some terrible aberration from normality but rather another way of being fully and wholly human (Swain and French, 2008). I would extend that idea further still and argue that such diverse experiences and identities can not only be fulfilling and enriching for the individuals affected, but can also enrich and enhance the life of wider society too. It is this approach to perceiving disability that I intend to present in this chapter, arguing that its adoption into the value base of the caring professions is one that could greatly enhance their ability to work more successfully in alliance with disabled people. This is particularly relevant too in the current era where an increasing emphasis is being placed on personalised service provision – a model of service design which has its origins in the disabled people's movement and the social model of disability.

I will begin by outlining the origins and development of the social model of disability, focusing in particular on the way that it has challenged the deficit-based view of disability dominated by bio-medicine, a view which underpins the widely held perception of disability as tragic. It is necessary to understand this background before we go on to look at the emergence of an 'affirmative model of disability' and to better understand the arguments on which it is based. It is these arguments, and their implications for practice in social work and social care, that will form the basis of the rest of the chapter.

The origins and development of the social model of disability

For much of the twentieth century the idea that disability was a purely bio-medical phenomenon, equivalent in most respects to disease and thus in need of similar programmes of eradication and treatment, went unquestioned. From this perspective the role of the caring professions and services was viewed as a natural and rational response to the 'pathological problem' of disability. A more critical view emerged in the 1960s and 1970s, however, developing the idea that the caring professions can also be seen as privileged groups engaged in pursuing their own material advancement and status, rather than working selflessly on behalf of their clients and/or patients (Abbott and Meerabeau, 1998). This was a theme taken up by theorists of the social model of disability. Although there are variations, a central tenet of the social model is the idea that the caring professions have often operated in a parasitic way, constructing bodies of knowledge and expertise based, not on the lived experience and desires of disabled people, but on allegedly expert perspectives derived from a bio-medical view of disability (e.g. Davies, 1993; Swain, et al., 2003).

This challenge to the dominance of the bio-medical perspective led to the recognition of new perspectives on the lived experience of disability in which many aspects of professional perception and practice were questioned, culminating in a challenge, led by the independent living movement among physically disabled people, to the whole idea of what disability is and how it should be defined. In 1976 the Union of the Physically Impaired Against Segregation (UPIAS, cited in Oliver, 1996) published a new definition of disability which replaced the term 'disability' with the term 'impairment' to describe the actual functional limitation experienced by an individual, while the meaning of 'disability' was altered to describe the limitations imposed on people with impairments by a society which fails to organise itself to meet their needs. Disability was therefore redefined as a category of social oppression in a similar way to that associated with categories of gender and race (Oliver, 1996).

Early versions of the social model focused strongly on the way people with impairments were excluded from paid employment and forced into dependence on welfare benefits and the caring professions and services and thus 'disabled' in the process (e.g. Oliver, 1993). Subsequently, greater emphasis was given to cultural as well as material factors. From this perspective disability is identified as a social construct, shaped by the social and cultural context within which it exists. This approach has focused on cultural representations of disability and disabled people and has shown how disability and deformity are frequently associated with evil, madness and even criminality in many cultures. Darke (1998), for example, has analysed the various ways in which disability is depicted in western cinema. A particularly good illustration of this in action may be found in the *Batman* films where most of the villains start as physically and psychologically normal, but end up as mentally bitter, twisted and criminally insane, often as a result of becoming physically and tragically distorted in some way. The root of such depictions lie, it can be argued, in the negativity associated with a bio-medical model that associates disability with the supposed evils of sickness, illness and deformity, a view often accepted uncritically among health, social care and even educational professionals. These professions have consequently created bodies of knowledge and expertise based on strong assumptions of tragedy, abnormality and pathology, reflected in practices which have tended to deprive disabled people of control and influence over what happens to them, while holding their whole lives up for scrutiny and reducing their identities to the status of 'cases' (Gillman, et al., 1997).

A major aim of this type of social constructionist analysis has been to understand and challenge the negative assumptions that dominate widely held views of disability, and to lay the ground for new, self-created identities for disabled people from which to challenge oppressive perceptions and practices. This has led to the emergence of what Brandon and Elliot (2008) have described as a culture of resistance among disabled people, one manifestation of which is the affirmative model of disability.

ACTIVITY **5.1**

Can you think of other media depictions of disabled people? What about cartoons and children's stories? If you can't think of many, what do you make of their absence?

Comment

A good deal has been written about the negative and simplistic stereotyping of women and black people in many forms of media, but rather less about how disabled people are portrayed. It is worth thinking about how this shapes all our attitudes and assumptions. It is interesting to contrast this with the artistic work described later in this chapter, which functions much more as acts of resistance and the assertion of a positive identity.

The affirmative model of disability

In a recent interview in the *New Scientist,* Stephen Hawking, widely recognised as one of the world's leading theoretical physicists and mathematicians and also severely physically impaired by the progression of motor neurone disease, is quoted as arguing that his condition has been *a blessing*, allowing him to focus on the intense intellectual activity that has made him one of the world's leading scientists, hugely extending human understanding of the universe as a result (George, 2009). Although Hawking himself has not to my knowledge advocated an affirmative model of disability, this quote could well be seen as an example of this model in action – the idea that the condition experienced by a disabled person is seen, not as a disaster, where they automatically assume a passive and dependent existence, living some kind of half-life that perhaps imitates but can never capture the fullness of normality. Instead, the condition itself is seen as allowing, or even liberating, the person to be more fully themselves, and as a platform from which to make their own unique contribution to their own life, and to society as a whole.

The affirmative model of disability is particularly associated with the work of Swain and French (2008), and it is they who have given it its strongest and fullest articulation so far. Their approach is based on the observation that, ... *while tragedy [is] the dominant view of disability and impairment, the writings of disabled people [express] a far more varied and positive picture*. The affirmative model, they assert,

> ... *is a way of thinking that directly challenges presumptions about the experiences, lifestyles and identities of people with impairments. Throughout history and in most cultures disabled people have been viewed as inferior, dangerous, tragic, pathetic and not quite human.*
>
> (2008, p65)

This negativity has been so powerful and pervasive that it has been, and continues to be used, to justify pre-natal screening programmes, abortion up to full term in pregnancy, and arguments for sterilisation and euthanasia as means to eradicate disability. Swain and French argue that *Affirmation is expressed through resilience and resistance to the dominant personal tragedy model* (2008, p65).

Case studies

Although the idea of an affirmative model of disability is a recent one, there are one or two precedents for this approach. One of particular note was the pioneering Know Me As I Am project conducted by Dorothy Atkinson and Fiona Williams (1990). This project was designed to capture the voices and experiences of people with learning difficulties through the medium of a variety of literary and artistic work. Much of this work relates and describes experiences of oppression, discrimination and prejudice, but what is striking also is how much is celebratory, telling stories of the pleasures of love, music and art, and a determination to enjoy life and live it to the full. At the time this was a radical perspective indeed, and one that many non-disabled people were not used to hearing. As we shall see later, however, literature and art have served as a significant medium for promoting an affirmative identity for disabled people.

A more recent example, reported by Trivedi (2009) is the Autistic Pride movement organised by people affected by the Autistic Spectrum Disorder (ASD) in the United States, who, basing their approach on the example of the gay pride movement, campaign publicly for 'autistic pride' under the slogan 'acceptance not cure'. The web-based organisation 'Aspies for Freedom' (Aspies is short for Asperger's syndrome – a form of ASD with relatively mild symptoms) campaigns for ASD to be seen as part of the broad range of human diversity rather than as a disease in need of a cure. They argue that support for people with ASD should be educational rather than medical, and that many of the behaviours and characteristics of ASD should be re-examined for their positive rather than problematic potential, or even as talents waiting to be channelled positively with appropriate support.

One activist has, for example, used the fact that he finds social situations difficult and stressful to cultivate his interest in martial arts and Buddhism, living a quasi-monastic lifestyle in which his desire for solitude is a positive advantage rather than a problem. Another example is that of Professor Temple Grandin, a leading animal scientist at

Colorado State University, whose deep, some might say obsessive, interest in cattle squeeze chutes led her to develop a highly successful career designing cattle management equipment in abattoirs – benefiting herself, the multi-million dollar cattle-handling industry in the USA, and improving the standard of animal welfare in the process.

A further example of an individual affected by a more severe form of ASD is Stephen Wiltshire, a young London-based man whose spectacular ability to draw striking images of buildings and cityscapes after only a very brief time spent observing them has, with some dynamic and entrepreneurial support, been turned into a highly successful artistic career. Stephen Wiltshire now has his own gallery, and sells paintings, prints and books around the world.

This way of looking at ASD is not uncontroversial, however, with some parents of children who are more seriously affected arguing that it might be all right for people with relatively mild forms of ASD, or for those with obvious exceptional abilities like Stephen Wiltshire, but for those with more severe and debilitating symptoms a medically orientated search for treatment and cure is still the most desirable approach. This is an important point and I will return to it later, but for the moment I want to stay with the 'affirmative' argument.

An important part of the approach highlighted above is the way that the idea of self-advocacy has been extended a stage further than usual. The self-advocacy movement for people with intellectual impairments – including people with ASD – has a long and proud tradition of campaigning for rights, advancement and protection from discrimination and prejudice stretching back into the 1970s and beyond (Walmsley, 2002). The ASD movement described above takes things a stage further than usual, however, arguing that at least some of the attributes of ASD can and should be regarded positively: characteristics to be affirmed and even celebrated, rather than regarded as problems or pathologies. It is this affirmative and celebratory emphasis that marks out the affirmative model of disability – bringing with it echoes of similar celebratory movements among the black, women's and gay pride movements.

Evidence review

As yet there is little or no research into the affirmative model of disability, but Brandon and Elliott (2008) have provided us with a useful overview of developments in the disability arts movement – a major source of affirmative ideas. They point out that there is evidence to support the idea that artistic and also scientific and other forms of creativity are often strongly linked to mental ill health, citing examples such as William Blake, Sylvia Plath, Earnest Hemingway and, more recently, Kurt Cobain. They also highlight the example of the survivors movement which has challenged the punitive and oppressive nature of traditional psychiatric services and treatments, using the slogan 'hugs not drugs'. They go on to cite the example of the 2007 TV documentary *The Secret Life of the Manic Depressive* by comedian, writer and actor Stephen Fry in which a number of other well-known people, including Robbie Williams, Jo Brand, Tony Slattery, Richard Dreyfus and Carrie Fisher, were interviewed about their experience of living with bipolar depressive disorder. The affirmative aspect arises from Fry's insistence that, despite its undisputed negative aspects, living with this condition is also what makes him who he is – so much so that, even if offered the opportunity of a cure, he wouldn't take it.

The suicides of Plath, Hemingway and Cobain do raise a serious question as to whether their particular examples can be used to advocate a celebration of the conditions from which they suffered – even if we can celebrate the work they produced. However, this in itself might also serve to illustrate the wider point at issue here, by raising the question of what might be the outcome for affected individuals if such conditions were more widely accepted and responded to as part of human diversity rather than pathologised and automatically assumed to be a disaster. Brandon and Elliot point out that such a perspective carries strong echoes of the work of the radical psychiatrist R D Laing in the 1960s who questioned why mental illness could not be viewed as a 'breakthrough' rather than a 'breakdown', and argued for a response based on using it as an opportunity to promote personal growth.

Brandon and Elliot (2008) also highlight the importance of distinguishing between art and writing that emerges from disabled people by their own design and motivation, rather than art that is driven by professional therapists for whom art is akin to a form of treatment for tragically affected individuals. Although they recognise that art-focused activities can be used in therapeutic ways, they focus instead on art that, whether produced by individuals working alone or by collective groups, is part of the culture of resistance from which a new self-defined identity is created. Among the examples they cite is the Lawnmowers Theatre Group in Gateshead, a group of people with learning diffi-culties who have written and produced performances satirising the *Valuing People* White Paper (DoH, 2001b); a similar group called Heart 'n Soul is based in London. There is also the Waddington Street Writers Group, a group of disabled writers who produce narratives and stories about their lives and experiences as both an artistic and a political act, and also the famous limbless statue of Alison Lapper in Trafalgar Square, which, like her own stage performances on which the statue was based, was designed to challenge stereotypes of beauty and perfection.

What all these examples have in common is the way in which art and performance is consciously used to establish a distinct disability counter-culture in which the artists not only challenge the dominant tragedy-based view of disability, but also work to establish a proud and positive identity for themselves, both individually and collectively. The strength and purpose of this cultural activity is summarised well by Neath and Schriner (1998) when they describe how it works to establish:

> ... a kinship based on identification of shared understandings of common life experiences ... to enable a sense of connectedness that can break down the feelings of isolation and alienation that stem from the belief that disability is a personal tragedy which necessarily excludes the disabled person from full social participation ... it provides a space within which positive identities can be constructed.

> (Cited in Brandon and Elliot, 2008, p100)

Implications for practice

Towards new ways of working using an affirmative model approach

So where does an affirmative model of disability take us in terms of practice in social work and social care? I would argue that adopting this approach could offer significant opportunities to work in ways that align with some of the highest aspirations of a caring and empowering professionalism, particularly in an era where the personalisation of service and support systems is high on the agenda. As noted above, professions are often looked at critically, but they can also be viewed positively.

For example, professionalism can be seen as a benchmark of performance, competence and moral quality. Friedson (1994), for example, has argued that 'professionalism' naturally reflects wider socio-cultural ideologies about the nature of professional competence, knowledge and morality. In his view, professions are, despite all the critiques, better than the alternatives, and are both necessary and desirable to maintain a decent society. Leonard (1997) has argued that the emancipatory project of the welfare state and the professions that inhabit it can be rediscovered only by acknowledging the powerful role of discourse as a form of cultural production of identity and knowledge systems. In particular, there is a need to acknowledge and celebrate, rather than pathologise and denigrate difference (Swain, et al., 2003).

Affirmative strategies in practice

The idea of developing new kinds of professionalism which attempt to address and overcome the shortcomings of traditional paternalistic approaches has been around for some time. Stacey (1992), for example, argued for a new professionalism focused on the ideal of service rather than expertise and control. Others have argued for a shift in the relationship between caring professionals and their clients. Beresford and Trevillion (1995), for example, as we shall see below, argue for a new form of professionalism, built on constructing a culture of collaboration. The key is turning this into effective actions. Any attempt to do this should focus on the following strategies.

A dialogue-based approach

A dialogue-based approach will draw heavily from the experience and expertise of individual service users and service user groups. In practice examples this kind of approach will focus on working with individuals to construct joint narratives about their health, lives and social situations, an approach designed to help them to name and claim their own experience, and help their carers and supporters to perceive them, not merely as 'cases', but as individuals with their own life stories, experiences, hopes and aspirations. Assessment and evaluation processes offer ideal opportunities to work in this way, but this approach should not be limited to these processes. The research referred to earlier by Gillman, et al. (1997) is a good example of this kind of work in practice, as is the 'lifemapping' work of Gray and Ridden (1999), the dialogue-based work of Ramcharan (1997) and the case studies described in my own work relating to people with learning difficulties and challenging behaviours (Goble, 2000). Such an approach can also have a transforming effect on professional consciousness and practice, fostering a psychology of interdependence (McGee and Menolacino, 1991).

A strengths and abilities focus

The case studies cited above illustrate the potential of using a strengths and abilities rather than a deficit and disability approach to supporting disabled people. Theorists of the social model of disability have argued that people are disabled when disabling barriers are constructed, either literally, as in the built environment with misplaced stairs, heavy doors, high pavements, etc., or in the social and cultural environment, reflected in negative views and perceptions about disabled people that result in them being denied opportunities to work, education or access to leisure and cultural activities – usually without even exploring whether and how this might be possible (Oliver, 1996). It has taken anti-discriminatory legislation to challenge these views and practices and enshrine the principle of such access as a right (DoH, 1995). Social work and social care professionals need to move beyond merely conforming to legal requirements, however. Using the dialogue-based approaches referred to above they need to work with disabled people to actively explore and identify those strengths and abilities which can be used and cultivated to identify and create opportunities – and also identify and challenge disabling barriers where they exist. This may well mean challenging our own perceptions about what a strength and an ability might look like. For example, being 'confined' to a wheelchair might actually be perceived as an advantage by someone who is interested in developing their knowledge and skills in the use of computer-based technologies. And in a knowledge-based economy there are many opportunities to use such skills to develop career and business, not to mention cultural and leisure, opportunities.

It is perhaps forgotten, for example, that we owe much of the development of the social model of disability itself to the pioneering work of teachers, researchers and theorists with physical, sensory and intellectual impairments who were enabled to work in universities and research units, and more recently for government departments, by challenging those institutions to transform their physical environments and by using modern information and communication technologies. Care professionals have often thought of independence for disabled people as being built around self-care skills such the ability to wash, dress and feed themselves. Many disabled people might well regard these as best performed quickly and safely with skilled and sensitive assistance rather than struggled through with difficulty on their own. Real independence comes from actually having control over who does this, when and where, and fitting it into the routines of a wider working and social life. Social care professionals need to enter into a dialogue with individual clients, explore and identify what is important to them, and help them build their own individually tailored plan of support and help to allow them to access opportunities and overcome disabling barriers.

Creating a collaborative culture

Building a collaborative culture requires a focus on the communication skills which will help to develop trust and good relationships with other professionals, organisations, clients themselves and their families, carers and relatives. Such skills are at the centre of the affirmative approach which we need to develop in planning, designing and providing support for clients. In their pioneering research Beresford and Trevillion (1995) placed commitment to the involvement of clients at the centre of their strategy for creating a collaborative culture and practice. They identified a number of key components to achieving this, including:

- allowing the space and time for such involvement – dependent on whatever level the client is able or willing to be involved;

- a commitment to including the client or their advocate or representative in decision making at *all* levels, including – and especially – those around important life choices and aspirations;

- avoidance of the use of professional jargon, and keeping technical language to its appropriate context;

- and finally a commitment not to sacrifice individual or collective client interests in inter-professional power play, point scoring or disputes, but rather to be led by the needs and aspirations of clients.

ACTIVITY **5.2**

In general terms you should be able to see a link between the three affirmative strategies above and many of the occupational standards you have to meet. Have a look either at those listed at the beginning of this chapter or the full details at www.gscc.org.uk/codes/. Try to make some explicit links, noting how adopting affirmative strategies will enable you to be a better social worker.

Comment

Here are some parts of the occupational standards that seem to me to link to what I have been arguing, though there are others.

1. *Communication skills and information sharing* – particularly:

    g. … Listen accurately to what individuals, families, carers, groups and communities have to say; …

    i.   Involve individuals, carers, groups and communities in decision making;

    j.   Offer individuals, carers, groups and communities choices and options;

    l.   Build honest relationships based on clear communication.

2. *Good social work practice* – particularly:

    d. Recognise the expertise of individuals, carers, groups and communities about their own situation and have regard for their wishes;

    e. Involve individuals, carers, groups and communities in all meetings which may affect them; …

    h. Assess needs properly:

        - making sure that all options are explored before embarking on a plan;
        - looking for options when the services needed are not available;
        - being creative.

C H A P T E R   S U M M A R Y

In this chapter I have sought to present and promote an affirmative model of disability. Central to this model is a challenge to the widely held view, with its origins in a deficit orientated bio-medical model, that the experience of disability is necessarily tragic. While strongly advocating for this affirmative model, I feel that it would be remiss of me to leave that argument without giving recognition to the fact that there are experiences of impairment and disability that can indeed be tragic. The long-distance lorry driver who suddenly loses his livelihood as a result of spinal injury; the parent of a child with a degenerative condition who sees their child develop and grow up normally into young adulthood, but then has to watch as they progressively lose physical, cognitive and sensory functioning; or the child who endures long, repetitive treatments to control a painful genetically related skin disorder, are all examples that demonstrate the point.

Even where people themselves experience their impairment in a positive way, there can be others around them who do not. In the article cited earlier where Stephen Hawking affirms his own positive take on his experience of life with motor-neurone disease, his daughter states:

> ... I think any relative of someone with a profound disability would wish away that disability if they could, because you witness an awful lot of suffering and a huge struggle.

> (George, 2009, p25)

This is a perspective echoed too by parents of children with severe forms of Autistic Spectrum Disorder, who argue that while an affirmative approach may be all right for people with relatively mild forms of ASD, their own experience of their child's suffering prompts them to keep up the pressure to find psychological and medical treatments and, ultimately, a cure (Trivedi, 2009). Such experiences need, in my view, to be recognised, validated and responded to in their own terms, and my aim has not been to deny or invalidate them, merely to point out that they are not the *only* way in which disability can be perceived or experienced. The important thing that such perspectives remind us of is the need to recognise the huge diversity and range of experience that arises from disability, and for the need to avoid the assumption that it is always going to be tragic in nature.

*FURTHER
READING*

Atkinson, D and Williams, F (eds) (1990) *Know me as I am: An anthology of prose, poetry and art by people with learning difficulties*. London: Hodder & Stoughton.

Probably still the best published example of this approach.

Swain, J and French, S (2008) *Disability on equal terms*. London: Sage.

Still the best published example of this approach.

As stated above, this is still a relatively new and under-researched area, but the work of John Swain and Sally French, arguably the main architects of this approach, is a very good place to start.

Chapter 6
Learning disabilities

Janet McCray

A C H I E V I N G   A   S O C I A L   W O R K   D E G R E E

This chapter will help you meet the following National Occupational Standards.

Key Role 1: Prepare for, and work with individuals, families, carers, groups and communities to assess their needs and circumstances.

- Prepare for social work contact and involvement.
- Work with individuals, families, carers, groups and communities to help them make informed decisions.

Key Role 2: Plan, carry out, review and evaluate social work practice, with individuals, families, carers, groups, communities and other professionals.

- Interact with individuals, families, carers, groups and communities to achieve change and development and to improve life opportunities.

Key Role 3: Support individuals to represent their needs, views and circumstances.

- Advocate with, and on behalf of, individuals, families, carers, groups and communities.

Key Role 6: Demonstrate professional competence in social work practice.

- Research, analyse, evaluate and use current knowledge of best social work practice.

It will also introduce you to the following academic standards as set out in the social work subject benchmark statement.

5.1.1 Social work services, service users and carers.

- Explanations of the links between definitional processes contributing to social differences (for example, social class, gender, ethnic differences, age, sexuality and religious belief) to the problems of inequality and differential need faced by service users.
- The nature of social work services in a diverse society (with particular reference to concepts such as prejudice, interpersonal, institutional and structural discrimination, empowerment and anti-discriminatory practices).

5.1.3 Values and ethics.

- The moral concepts of rights, responsibility, freedom, authority and power inherent in the practice of social workers as moral and statutory agents.

5.5.3 Analysis and synthesis.

- Assess the merits of contrasting theories, explanations, research, policies and procedures.
- Critically analyse and take account of the impact of inequality and discrimination in work with people in particular contexts and problem situations.

Introduction

The Learning Disability Task Force notes that good progress has been made in tackling the inequality of people with learning disabilities since the publication of *Valuing people* in 2001 (DoH, 2001b, 2007). Recently there has been fresh interest in the original report and its contents, as the emphasis on personalised and self-directed support gains impetus in *Valuing people now: the delivery plan* (DoH, 2009b). Personalised support means that people plan, organise and set up their own provision (DoH, 2008a, 2008b) using input from agencies as required.

Such developments are already having a positive psychological impact on people with learning disabilities and their carers (Manthorpe, et al., 2009), while research by people with learning disabilities themselves (Hart, et al., 2007, p1) suggests that the more choices that were available to people the more likely they were to be included in local communities and services.

Despite services moving in the right direction, this group of people remain at risk of devaluation and consequently are more likely to be marginalised in society (DoH, 2007), while Mir, et al. (2001, p2) note that people from ethnic minorities with learning disabilities experience simultaneous disadvantage in relation to race, impairment and, for women, gender.

So while moves toward personalised care and self-directed support give more people choice about how they receive care and from whom, it is important to highlight that, so far, services have not recognised the diverse needs of black and ethnic minority people who may have had difficulty accessing information on self-directed support.

As a social worker building partnerships with minority ethnic people who have learning disabilities you need the knowledge, skills and values in practice to work positively and effectively. This chapter will support you in making judgements about the appropriateness of services. The chapter's content will define valued practice and what its attributes are, discussing what is meant by being non-judgemental and also exploring stereotypes and assumptions about models of support for minority ethnic people (Evans and Banton, 2001) and how to address them, through developing culturally specific practice, tackling oppression and discrimination, and using advocates or brokers (Chahal and Ullah, 2004). You will be guided to enable people with learning disabilities to gain access to information about individualised payments through understanding monocultural barriers and how to overcome them. Throughout the chapter emphasis will focus on involving people actively in changing or designing models of support, while also recognising both the multiple identities people hold, like ethnicity, disability, heritage, class and gender (Singh, 2005), and the multiple oppressions people with learning disability face, including social exclusion, poverty and isolation (Joint Committee on Human Rights, 2008, p9). In the chapter the term 'learning disability' – used in most policy documents – will be used to describe people with a learning disability or learning difficulty.

Defining valued practice

In 2004, the International Federation of Social Workers (IFSW) produced a *Code of ethics for valued practice*, as follows:

1. *Respecting the right to self-determination* Social workers should respect and promote people's rights to make their own choices and decisions, irrespective of their values and life choices, provided this does not threaten the rights and legitimate interests of others.

2. *Promoting the right to participation* Social workers should promote the full involvement and participation of people using their services in ways that enable them to be empowered in all aspects of decisions and actions affecting their lives.

3. *Treating each person as a whole* Social workers should be concerned with the whole person, within the family, community and societal and natural environments, and should seek to recognise all aspects of a person's life.

4. *Identifying and developing strengths* Social workers should focus on the strengths of all individuals, groups and communities and thus promote their empowerment.

All social workers should sign up to these attributes and see them as central to their practice, as they should the GCSC code of practice cited in the opening chapter and at the start of each subsequent chapter. These can act as a guide when wishing to work positively with people from ethnic minority backgrounds who have learning disabilities. For example, if we think about *treating each person as an individual*, a starting point is being non-judgemental and addressing stereotypes and assumptions about people. Cranmer and McCray (2009, p88) explore stereotyping in relation to collaborative practice with service users in the Learning Matters text *Working with vulnerable adults*. Additionally working to the code of practice will help guide you through the goals of personalised care.

Defining personalised care

Carr and Dittrich (2008, p4) define personalisation in adult services as:

- finding new collaborative ways of working and developing local partnerships, which produce a range of services for people to choose from and opportunities for social inclusion;

- tailoring support to people's individual needs;

- recognising and supporting carers in their role while enabling them to maintain a life beyond their caring responsibilities;

- a total system response so that universal and community services and resources are accessible to everyone;

- early intervention and prevention so that people are supported early on and in a way that's right for them.

As you can see the concept of personalisation means a very different way of both viewing and responding to people's needs. At its core personalisation recognises an individual's right to influence, participate in and, if desired, manage the planning and delivery of their care, a move from a one-size-fits-all model of service design to an individual, unique response. A number of terms are used to describe personalisation, and Glasby (2009, p28) notes confusion around their meanings. Personalisation may include:

- direct payments for social care where an individual after assessment is offered a means-tested financial allowance to purchase his or her own care and support (Carr and Dittrich, 2008, p6);

- individual budgets which incorporate a number of resources from different funding streams which people can use to gain a mix of services and payment to organise care to suit themselves. This can be paid directly to the person, but not all individuals can or wish to organise this funding so a range of facilitation methods are in place such as *through a care manager, by a trust, as an indirect payment to a third party such as a broker or held by a service provider* (Carr and Dittrich, 2008, p8).

The principles and practice of personalisation should mean that the days of monocultural service provision for people with learning disability from Black and ethnic minority populations is diminishing. Current research shows that this may not yet be the case. Respondents to the consultation on *Valuing people now* (DoH, 2009b, p6) noted that *service providers, commissioners and policy makers were not specifically addressing the needs of people with more complex needs and people from black and minority ethnic groups and newly arrived communities.* While the Joint Committee on Human Rights (JCHR) records:

> A recurring theme in the evidence was the lack of easy to understand, illustrated
> information to enable people with learning disabilities (most of whom have some
> difficulties with reading) to have more choice and control over their everyday
> lives. If people with learning disabilities are really to enjoy life like other people, as
> Government policy intends, then they also need easy to understand information on all
> the issues related to day-to-day living such as health, housing, benefits, employment,
> crime and safety.
>
> (2008, p87)

RESEARCH SUMMARY

Findings on barriers to valued practice

The Audit Commission (2004) reports that to promote diversity effectively we need to stop doing the things that create barriers and start doing the things that break them down. While there are positive examples of practice, there still remains a need for further development of new knowledge and skill to work effectively to meet individual need. Butt (2006, p7) assesses the impact of stereotyping, being judgemental and making assumptions about the needs of individuals and communities. He suggests that such responses are a result of institutional and direct discrimination (these issues are explored several times in this book). This is complex when support to people with learning disabilities from ethnic minority groups is observed, since the impact of racism may be attributed to the person's learning disability. An example would be when social workers, service providers, planners and commissioners in social care hold a view that informal or family support is always available for people with learning disability in minority ethnic populations and hence people look after their own (Butt, 2006, p7). This may mean services remain underdeveloped and that there are very real gaps in service delivery and support while people do not get their needs met and rights acknowledged (JCHR, 2008, p9). Butt

Continued

---

uses data from the 2001 census (ONS, 2004) to explore rates of disability and long-term illness among people from different ethnic groups in England. Evidence suggests that those in Black and minority ethnic groups have higher levels of disability and illness. If this is viewed along with the evidence of continuing disadvantage and discrimination that having a learning disability creates, then many individuals remain at very high risk of social exclusion (Walker and Northmore, 2005). The Valuing people now *paper (DoH, 2009b) does recognise this and has endorsed the development of regional and local action groups through learning Disability Partnership Boards and Family Carer Groups (DoH, 2009b, p6).*

Research evidence demonstrates that making assumptions about people's needs based on stereotypes perpetuates discrimination. If people are to access and design their own individual support, services need to change. Valued practice involves engagement with service users, and this includes having knowledge of specific communities (Quereshi, *et al.,* 2000), being an effective communicator and using appropriate techniques in order that people can articulate their needs, such as using sign language (Quereshi, *et al.,* 2000) and symbols (Ahmed, 1998) to communicate. It is also vital that clear information is available (Butt and Dhaliwal, 2005).

Components of culturally specific practice

Valued practice means that as a social worker you will be supporting an individual and their family and/or network to get the services they want. To support people from minority ethnic backgrounds with learning disabilities you will need to both understand and develop culturally specific practice skills. This means taking a good look at your perspectives on practice and what an individual might require from you and/or a service and then reflecting on what values and experience are driving these decision-making processes. If you would like to know more about the skills of reflection, the text *Reflective practice in social work* (Knott and Scragg, 2007) also in the Learning Matters series will help you. As Parton and O'Byrne (2000) observe *we cannot assume that our ways of understanding are necessarily the same as others in society*. So, for example, a white older male social worker may have a very different view to a young Black male with a learning disability about what his needs are and how they could be met. A number of factors might influence this difference. An important point is not to make assumptions about what the needs are and how they could be addressed.

Donovan is a 23-year-old young Black man with a learning disability living in a provincial town in England. Donovan currently lives with his mother who provides much of his care and support following his return home after spending some time at a residential boarding school between the ages of 12 and 16. In the last two years, Donovan's life has become less social and more isolated as his older sister has moved from the family home to her

Continued

own flat while his brother is now at university. Donovan also has limited opportunity to go out, saying that the day centre is aimed at an older group of people and he does not want to attend. At night, as his mother works shifts, a neighbour often provides informal support and watches TV with Donovan.

Donovan's mother is soon to have an operation and has contacted you as Donovan's social worker about additional support needs while she is recuperating. As his social worker your original priority was to organise this, but on meeting Donovan briefly you find that there may be other needs not currently being addressed.

ACTIVITY **6.1**

Think about your role as Donovan's social worker and any factors which might influence decisions you make about addressing his needs. Write these down.

Consider any assumptions you might have made about Donovan's disability, race or age. What are they based upon?

Comment

Research by Carr and Robbins (2009, p6) shows that a number of dominant themes influence social workers not to offer direct payments to people who use services. They note that front-line workers are often not aware of the direct payments policy or they may consider people on their caseload too vulnerable or at risk for them to give consent appropriately. Further, Carr and Robbins write that care managers may be reluctant to offer direct payments to some service users because of resource issues (2009, p6). Citing the work of Neely-Barnes, et al. (2008) they suggest that for people with learning disabilities a two-tier system may be in operation where people with more severe learning disability were less likely to live in their home and have choices about their lifestyles.

Black and minority ethnic people who use services may also not have had full information on what direct payments are or how to gain access to appropriate information in order to make choices (Stuart, 2006). The impact of these barriers will be significantly increased if you are Donovan, with a learning disability and Black. The paper *Nothing about us without us* (DoH, 2001a) notes: *Social services need to provide adequate information and support to people with learning disabilities to use Direct Payments if they wish.*

As a social worker you may well be aware of some of these issues for individuals with learning disability. To avoid these barriers being maintained and reinforced it is important to take a good look at the responses you make to individuals like Donovan and what these are based upon. Positive practice involves developing culturally specific skills and an awareness of the limitations and discrimination that monocultural (i.e. aimed primarily at a white population) service delivery (Chahal and Ullah, 2004, p4) can create.

In order to make sure you practise positively you need to be clear about your knowledge and skills. For example, do you know about your authority's use of individual payments?

Are you aware of the support offered to enable people to have and make choices? What is the local community like, its ethnic, religious, gender and age profile? How good are partnership links with third and independent sector community organisations for Black and minority ethnic people? To support Donovan effectively what do you know about young adult community activity in the area? Are you confident and capable of responding to the needs of individual Black and minority ethnic people in terms of language, gender and cultural needs (Chahal and Ullah, 2004, p7)? If you are confident about your responses to these initial questions then you are ready to answer the following question.

ACTIVITY 6.2

What action would you need to undertake to ensure that any needs identified are shared by Donovan?

Communication with Donovan is vital. Equally important is communication with his mother and other key family supports. In this context Donovan's neighbour has a vital role in Donovan's life. It may well be your first full formal visit to Donovan so it is important not to make assumptions about what's needed. Other professionals and agencies may be a part of Donovan's family support or history. Further, as Donovan's mother may be seeking an immediate solution to the short-term care of Donovan while she is in hospital this may be her only current focus. Working through potential new models of support and delivery will take time so cannot be hurried. The family may not have heard of personalisation or what it could offer them in the future. At this stage your enthusiasm could be viewed positively in actively seeking them out to provide information or it may seem intrusive, dominant and based on your values. You could be creating uncertainty (Owen and Farmer, 1995) rather than being helpful.

Ask yourself what Donovan's preferred style of communication is – for example verbal and written, signs and symbols, technological or a more individual approach – and work from there. If Donovan had a hearing impairment it would be important to check carefully on the type of sign language used by people in his ethnic group (Namaganda, 2004). Are there publications or web links available that might help Donovan and his family access further information? The JCHR cites the Cambridgeshire Parliament of People with Learning Disabilities who note: *We need to know the same information as everyone else, but we need to have it broken down and with pictures* (2008, p83, para 222).

As a social worker have you viewed these publications or websites to ensure they are not monocultural in approach and message? Would offering this type of information be culturally appropriate? Brooks, et al. (2000) observe that information translated straight from English may not make sense in some languages and note that one English word can sometimes be a full sentence once translated. If you don't feel experienced enough to make this judgement you can use advice from your organisation's trained interpreters or translators to inform your decisions.

Do Black and minority ethnic service user and family or advocacy networks exist in the area which could offer vital personal experience of direct payments to Donovan and his family? If you know of groups, would they be appropriate or would you be generalising too much, for example making assumptions about similarities between people in terms of language, values, culture and age (Clark, 2002)?

ACTIVITY **6.3**

As you work through your practice strategies for Donovan, draw up a list of your own strengths.

Comment

You may already be confident of your communication and assessment skills and knowledge, have good local information and be a member of a number of networks which are working to achieve the broad personalisation goals set out above. If you have new knowledge to learn, identify how you intend to gain and apply this as part of your practice placement experience. At this point your next steps are vital in ensuring that you do not, through inadvertent behaviour, demonstrate individual racism. For example, if you were to prejudge or ignore Donovan's ethnic minority background and offer services based on this view, it would have a racist impact upon him.

As you explore Donovan's situation and you find that the agency response you observe is concerned only with the needs of the larger white group's needs you should be aware of institutional racism in operation. When racism at both the individual, professional level and the organisational and agency level are present, these can further interact and legitimise prejudice (Bromley and Longino, 1972).

Influencing change

As a social worker you are key in influencing change in your organisation. In offering more personalised support there are a number of ways in which you are able to collaborate and influence changes in any current oppressive practice. For example, in terms of communication strategies with Black and minority ethnic groups, you might ask whether the organisation is using the culturally specific strategies of good practice outlined above, and if they are not doing so, for what reason? Are you familiar with access routes to current advocacy and support services in place for people to connect with? If there is no organisational attention given to these culturally sensitive elements of personalised support, you will need to act to begin to address the gaps. Ask yourself, if you do not act what are the consequences and impact? To what extent is it your individual responsibility? By thinking and acting smartly you can influence your organisation positively and begin to create change. Hall explores change through managing the self (Hall, 2009), and if you would like to read more on the topic of change see the further reading section below.

You may need to undertake some research to discover which audiences, networks and individual leaders you need to work in partnership with. Your focus should be on evaluating the results of your responses, and asking yourself if this is adequate or should you be doing more? As Flynn (2002) observes:

> *Black communities are tired of taking part in research that asks them what they want from services, only to find nothing happens until five years later when they are asked the same questions over again.*

(Cited in Chahal and Ullah, 2004, p9)

C H A P T E R   S U M M A R Y

This chapter has explored the potential of personalised support for people with learning disability from Black and minority ethnic backgrounds. You have read about the very real progress being made in service delivery for people with learning disability and how personalised provision may enhance this further. It is still the case that Black or minority ethnic people with any health or social care needs are under-represented in service delivery due to direct or indirect discrimination. This impacts when people are accessing direct payments or individual budgets, so active work still needs to be done to ensure that individuals and their families can participate in these schemes. Your reading will have enabled you to understand the need for engaging in valued social work practice to make this happen. This includes reflecting on your own current knowledge, skills and beliefs and how these may need to be developed. A key part of this process may have involved addressing some uncomfortable assumptions about your own current practice behaviours and your organisation's strategies for service delivery. Having faced these challenges and clarified your development needs you will be able to plan, influence and offer culturally sensitive support to facilitate people in making their own choices about what they need. A problem-focused approach will be needed that recognises and works positively to address – and where necessary act – to expose the underlying damage to individuals' lifestyles that discrimination can cause. From this position you will be working to reduce isolation (Chahal and Ullah, 2004, p8), achieve greater representation and play a positive part by working in an organisation which promotes the independence of people from groups that are frequently marginalised in society who also have learning disability.

FURTHER READING

Mantell, A (ed.) (2009) *Social work skills with adults*. Exeter: Learning Matters.
This book includes chapters on self-management and collaboration which are important for managing change in service delivery.

Martin, V (2003) *Leading change in health and social care*. Abingdon: Routledge.
This book explores leading change from a range of positions in social care organisations.

Chapter 7
Class

Gianna Knowles

ACHIEVING A SOCIAL WORK DEGREE

This chapter will help you meet the following National Occupational Standards.

Key Role 1: Prepare for, and work with individuals, families, carers, groups and communities to assess their needs and circumstances.
- Prepare for social work contact and involvement.
- Work with individuals, families, carers, groups and communities to help them make informed decisions.

Key Role 2: Plan, carry out, review and evaluate social work practice, with individuals, families, carers, groups, communities and other professionals.
- Interact with individuals, families, carers, groups and communities to achieve change and development and to improve life opportunities.

Key Role 3: Support individuals to represent their needs, views and circumstances.
- Advocate with, and on behalf of, individuals, families, carers, groups and communities.

Key Role 6: Demonstrate professional competence in social work practice.
- Research, analyse, evaluate and use current knowledge of best social work practice.

It will also introduce you to the following academic standards as set out in the social work subject benchmark statement.

5.1.1 Social work services, service users and carers.
- Explanations of the links between definitional processes contributing to social differences (for example, social class, gender, ethnic differences, age, sexuality and religious belief) to the problems of inequality and differential need faced by service users.
- The nature of social work services in a diverse society (with particular reference to concepts such as prejudice, interpersonal, institutional and structural discrimination, empowerment and anti-discriminatory practices).

5.1.3 Values and ethics.
- The moral concepts of rights, responsibility, freedom, authority and power inherent in the practice of social workers as moral and statutory agents.

5.5.3 Analysis and synthesis.
- Assess the merits of contrasting theories, explanations, research, policies and procedures.
- Critically analyse and take account of the impact of inequality and discrimination in work with people in particular contexts and problem situations.

Introduction: what do we mean by class?

Class is a challenging term to define. On the one hand it is sometimes used to determine certain economic or financial characteristics about a person or a group of people. On the other hand it can relate to the ways individuals and groups behave, the beliefs they hold and even the clothes they wear and the food they eat. This chapter will seek to explore some of these challenges, beginning by looking at traditional markers for class and why some people may be labelled working class or middle class. It will also discuss how class is used to describe different sets of values, attitudes and beliefs that different groups in society seem to hold. It will explore the relationship between class, low income and poverty and the knock-on effects of living in such situations. Finally it will seek to discuss the notion that there is a dominant middle-class culture in Britain that can be both a barrier to well-being for some and an enabler for others.

ACTIVITY 7.1

Would you describe yourself as being working class, middle class or upper class?

You may not have yet given much consideration to the notion of class, or what class you belong to. Conversely, you may have very strong views on the subject and be quite clear what class you belong to. Whatever the case, at this point in your reading, decide which class you believe you belong to and list five bullet points that support your reasons. If you take the position that there is no such thing as social class, list five reasons to support your point of view.

Comment

In some ways class is the most subjective of the social differences we deal with in this book, the one that is perceived to be more a matter of personal opinion than, say, age or disability (though neither of these are simple, objective categories either). While they might deny or affirm their effects, politicians don't say there is no such thing as religion or gender, nor do they suggest that by effort and hard work individuals can change their ethnicity. They do assert these things about class.

Determining class by economic factors

The term class has been around in Britain since the eighteenth century. However, it is mainly from the work of Karl Marx (1818–83), who was writing in the nineteenth century, that our current use of the term is still based. Marx was writing at a time when Britain had undergone huge social and economic change. In the space of 150 years it had moved from being a mainly agricultural economy to an industrial one. This change brought with it a great movement of people migrating into towns to look for work in factories and centres of industry – including coal mining and steel manufacturing.

The conditions endured by workers in industry at this time are now infamous. At its worst, appalling living conditions were experienced by hundreds of thousands in poorly sanitised slums, and whole families worked in factories and down mines in dangerous conditions.

In exploring why there seemed to be such a divide in society with the very rich industrial-ists on the one hand and the almost impoverished, powerless workers on the other, Marx argued that their relationship to what he called 'the means of production' was central (Wheen, 2000). It determined how rich or poor they might be and, therefore, what quality of life they might expect.

In very general terms what Marx meant is that there were those that owned or controlled factories, banks and other agencies that generated wealth – the means of production. If you were not part of this class and able to live by the wealth and profit it generated, then virtually the only way for you to make a living was to work in these industries, generating profit for others but living on far more meagre wages than your employers. In this way both classes needed each other to make the system work, but the class that owned the means of production were the more privileged class. It can be argued that for many reasons – changes in attitudes, the wider availability of free education and changes in employment law – people's situation now in relation to the means of production is very different, although some of Marx's analysis of the situation still applies.

Since the nineteenth century there has been a development of a middle class that does not directly own the means of production and live on profit from it but is necessary to manage the interface between workers and owners. The system needs this class to be well-educated and professional (we will come back to this idea again later) to enable appropriate, informed decisions to be made that will balance both the needs of the owners and, arguably, those of the workers. However, in many ways, this middle class seems to have more in common, in terms of wants, attitudes and aspirations, with the owning class rather than with manual workers.

Governments, particularly since 1945 with reforms of the education system and the development of welfare provision, have sought to make class mobility possible, enabling movement from the working class to the middle class (if not to the owning class). The significant growth in the size of the middle class during this period has led to various politicians, both from the right and the left, to comment *we are all middle class now* (Riddell, 1998). We know Britain has changed considerably since the nineteenth century, both in social and economic ways and in the reduced gulf between workers and factory owners. However, this chapter is arguing that class has not gone away and still matters in people's lives.

CASE STUDY

Gill is in her late 40s and a primary school teacher in the Midlands. She says:

I think of myself as being middle class now, but my parents were working class, well they started out working class, well ... my mother did anyway.

My mother's father – my grandfather – lost his father in the First World War, and his mother couldn't look after him and his brother, so he spent some of his child-hood in a Barnardo's home. He lied about his age to get into the army in the 30s, survived the war (his brother died in the Far East). After the war he joined the prison service, which meant he got a house too. My grandmother left school at

Continued

> ### CASE STUDY continued
>
> 13 and went to be a servant 'up at the big house'. They always lived in prison officers' accommodation until the 1980s when they were able to buy their council flat, although they had retired by then.
>
> My mum had to leave school at 16 as she was the eldest of three girls and they couldn't afford for her to stay on at school. She took A levels at night school and always worked in libraries. She was determined I would go to college, as it was then, and get a degree and have more opportunities than her.

> ### ACTIVITY 7.2
>
> *Would you agree with Gill's classification of herself as middle class and her parents as working class?*

Comment

While much of this discussion is about aspects of people's lives that are real in that they can be measured, it is worth remembering that social class distinctions are also in people's heads. Others may not think they are real, but if they affect social interaction they are real in their consequences.

Another way of explaining our current understanding of the term class is by looking at how the government and aspects of the media use it. Often the benchmarking they are using is that devised by the Office for National Statistics (ONS), the guidelines called the *Standard Occupational Classification 2000* (ONS, 2009). This classifies people according to the nature of their work and what their income is as a result of that employment. It is not unlike a modern equivalent of determining our relationship to the means of production. The nature of work is classified according to two criteria: the kind of work the individual is asked to perform (the job) and the competencies needed to perform the tasks and duties related to the job (skills) (ONS, 2009).

The *Standard Occupational Classification* (SOC) places all occupations in one of nine major categories, with subdivisions in each major category. The occupations listed are ranked, with those commanding the greatest socio-economic advantages at the top (those closest to controlling the country's wealth), with the less well paid, less socio-economically advantageous jobs at the bottom (those furthest away from control of the means of production, however necessary they may be in keeping the country on its feet). The nine major categories are listed below.

1. Managers and senior officials – top company, bank and government executives.

2. Professional occupations – doctors, lawyers, teachers, science and engineering professionals, public service professionals – including social workers, police officers (inspectors and above).

3. Associated professional and technical occupations – police officers (sergeant and below), nurses.

4. Administrative and secretarial occupations.

5. Skilled trade occupations – plumbers, electricians.

6. Personal service occupations – hairdressers, nursery nurses, sport and leisure workers.

7. Sales and customer service occupations – those working in shops.

8. Process, plant and machine operatives – factory work.

9. Elementary occupations – bar work, waiters, farm workers, postal workers, labouring work.

(ONS, 2009)

While the SOC does not use the terms middle class and working class, it is possible to map its nine major socio-economic categories onto the more traditional terms of working class and middle class, with the first two categories more or less matching common understandings of what middle class means (the upper or owning class being very small and beginning to appear in the most powerful of those in the first category).

A further distinction has historically been made in research (and probably in common-sense terms too) about whether a particular job is regarded as being manual, skilled or professional (Benson, 2003, p12), the criterion being whether some form of training is needed to do the job and to what level. Education to degree level is usually seen as the cut-off point between being a skilled worker and being in a profession, so being an electrician requires training and skills, whereas to be a social worker, a professional occupation, education to degree level is required. Underlying this distinction is the idea that to be skilled requires only the ability to know how to complete a task, whereas a profession is perceived as requiring a deeper understanding of issues. Where challenging decisions have to be taken, it requires more than craft skill to be able to make a sound judgement by reflecting on alternatives and applying reflective knowledge and understanding. Or so the argument goes.

These judgements are contestable, vary in different European countries, and shift over time. Nursing, for example, is to be an all-graduate profession from 2013 and in some localities education to degree level is preferred for applicants to the police service. Similarly, with the introduction of foundation degrees and top-up programmes, many of those in occupations below the second ONS category can undertake training to degree level yet might continue to be unrecognised as professionals.

Generally speaking, professional occupations command a higher income and more long-term benefits than skilled occupations, although this distinction has arguably been eroded in recent years. For example, one long-term benefit of being in a professional occupation used to be home ownership and usually an occupational as well as a state pension. However, home ownership is now available to a wider sector of the population (though it remains impossible for some) and all are encouraged to ensure some form of private pension (actually barely realistic for someone in low-paid work in areas with persistent unemployment).

Some will also argue that the once very marked financial distinction between classes seems to have narrowed, with some skilled workers being able to command incomes comparable to those with degree qualifications, and in comparison with a century ago this is true. However, this may only be short-lived. Someone who earns their money by selling a skill – such as plumbing or hairdressing – may reach the top level of their possible income quite quickly. A hairdresser can only deal with a finite number of clients in one day, even if they can charge clients top rates, and few plumbers in their 50s have the physical fitness that enabled them to earn what they did in their 30s. There is a related argument that while a few may become high-earning hairdressers to the stars or run their own exclusive salons, they are not as scarce as very experienced barristers. These too can only deal with a few clients at a time, but can charge very much more for doing so. Social workers come somewhere inbetween: at some point in their careers perhaps earning less than established hairdressers, but with the long-term advantage of a career structure supported by training, enabling them to progress to higher incomes. They will also have more secure pension benefits than any plumber.

Whereas some elements of the economic distinctions between the working class and the middle class have changed over the past few years, explaining class in purely financial terms tells only part of the story and this chapter will go on to look at other aspects of what is meant when we use the terms middle class and working class.

ACTIVITY 7.3

Reflecting on your response to the first activity – what class do you think you belong to – and given what you have read so far, have you changed your mind about your class or not?

Review the five bullet points you wrote to support your choice (or your rejection of the whole idea of class). Do you want to change, delete or add anything?

Comment

It may be worth rereading the final part of the opening chapter in sorting out your ideas on this. You may find friends and colleagues polarise here, either insisting there is such a thing as social class and being keen to tell you which they are in, or arguing completely the opposite.

Class cultures and cultural capital

So far this chapter has dealt with the notion of class in economic terms. However, how much people earn is not the only thing that impacts on the way they live their lives. Irrespective of how much money we have, we hold values, attitudes and beliefs that give meaning to our lives and the lives of those most immediate to us, particularly our family and friends but also the people we work with. *Culture is involved in all those practices ... which carry meaning for us* (Du Gay, 1997, p3). These cultural notions are fundamental to our concept of self and who we see ourselves as being, what we might call our identity.

While the cultural views we hold are usually influenced by those around us in our most formative years, they can also be influenced by the wider environment and community in which we have grown up, and by what we pick up from such sources as the media. This is not to say that we cannot make choices about what we wish to do and believe, but it is important to acknowledge the impact of these early influences.

For example, the traditional middle class view of education is to see it as a long-term investment, expecting that children should stay in education until they are 18 and probably beyond. Careers are also a long-term investment, so the social worker contrasted earlier with a hairdresser is more likely to take on a mortgage because of the expectation of a secure and progressively rising salary. Saving for pensions and investing surplus income in long-term savings schemes makes more cultural as well as economic sense in a secure profession.

We have already seen how economic factors can be the distinguishing factor in deciding who is working class and who might be middle class; it is often these factors that impact on the choices families make about their children's education and how income is spent. It may not be economically possible for someone from a home where income is low to pursue their education beyond the statutory school-leaving age. Or, the risk entailed in going to university and leaving with substantial debts and no guarantee of a professional job once one graduates is much harder to take after a childhood of economic uncertainty or poverty. Such attitudes are not necessarily entirely culturally specific to class but they are heavily influenced by income, which is a factor of class.

I may have many aspirations about what I want to do in life, but the class I belong to and particularly the resultant income may make it more difficult to for me to achieve those aspirations. Key elements of this are summarised by Wright, who observes that class

> ... *determines access to material resources ... shapes the mundane material conditions of existence – how comfortable is daily life, how physically and mentally taxing is work, how hungry one is. Class location significantly determines the probability of being the victim of different kinds of crime. Class locations shape the kind of neighborhood one is likely to live in and the nature of the social networks in which one is embedded.*

> (Wright, 2000, p202)

We know *people and their parents are influenced by the people and places where they live* (Cabinet Office, 2008, p15). We know that people who live in deprived areas have fewer aspirations for themselves and for their children than those who live in more affluent areas. Research suggests this is because:

> *In some deprived areas, people's social networks tend to be less wide ranging and neighbourhood characteristics such as housing, the local environment, crime rates and the quality of services, are also likely to influence their attitudes.*

> (Cabinet Office, 2008, p15)

Despite many claiming that we are all middle class now, we have seen how it is quite clearly not the case and not only are we *not* all middle class, but our class system is still a system that privileges one class above another. Or, as Adams, et al. (2007) suggest, some groups in society hold more economic and cultural power than other members of society and the dominance of those values, attitudes and beliefs prevent others from thriving. As Gramsci argues:

... a dominant group can so successfully project its particular way of seeing social reality that its view is accepted as common sense, as part of the natural order, even by those who are disempowered by it.

(Cited in Adams, et al., 2007, p10)

We have already seen how some jobs, such as being a social worker or a teacher, are commonly defined as professional middle-class occupations. It may also be argued that these occupations are not only (by definition) economically middle class, but those doing them are culturally middle class and this in turn sets up barriers to enabling those on low incomes to achieve well-being. There is a clash of cultures where the dominant class only recognises its own values as being those that have worth (hence the contempt for 'chavs'). An obvious challenge for social workers is therefore to resist the idea that there is only one set of correct class values and to acknowledge the complex issues most people deal with in their lives. We also shouldn't assume everyone can plan their lives in a way that ensures they always get better or are not subject to unexpected events, like those experienced by Clare and Mike in the case study below.

CASE STUDY

Clare and Mike have a four-year-old boy, Liam, who is disabled. Liam's condition means that he requires daily physiotherapy exercises and he is struggling to learn to communicate through speech. He becomes very frustrated and sometimes angry when he cannot help himself or make himself understood. When this happens his movements become jerky and he shouts out. He needs to wear a nappy, which requires changing throughout the day, and he needs help feeding himself. He loves football, he likes to watch it on television, to watch others playing it when he is taken out, and to look at football magazines and have someone sit with him and talk about pictures and the games he has watched. His wheelchair is in the colours of his favourite football team. He also loves animals and likes it when the family cat will sit on his lap.

Clare used to be an auxiliary nurse and was also taking her nursing diploma part-time when she became pregnant. She went on maternity leave to have Liam but gave up work after he was born and they realised the level of care he was likely to need. Mike has recently been made redundant from his job in a car factory that has just closed down. He got some redundancy pay, but since he had not been employed at the factory all that long what he received has now all gone. Because the factory used to employ most of the men in the area he is now one of many looking for another job. He has taken up some basic skills training, which he has been required to do to enable him to claim his unemployment benefit. He says it's more to give him something to do since he hasn't learnt anything he didn't learn at school.

The family have been provided with housing and it has been adapted for Liam. Clare says:

> The flat is really good, we got a lot of help with things like that when Liam was a baby and Mike was in work, so things were manageable, but now Liam's a little boy and Mike's unemployed it's getting more challenging. Liam's simply getting bigger and stronger and it gets harder to lift him around, to change his nappy, do his exercises, etc. and if he's not in the mood it's really hard. It worries me as I

Continued

CASE STUDY *continued*

can see it's going to be difficult as he gets even bigger. It's also been hard to find pre-school provision for him. Either places say they can't take him because they don't have the facilities or properly trained staff – even though there is money to support him. Or places are really enthusiastic, but haven't thought it through and can't cope as well as they thought and phone me up to come and sort him out. It's frustrating for him as well as for me, since you can't rely on anything and we're already worrying about getting him into a school.

Money is also a worry, we do get help because of Liam's condition, but the money barely covers his childcare and we can't get Working Tax Credit because neither of us are working, I could probably get some hours at the hospital, but I couldn't earn enough, given what we would lose in benefits, to make that work. And Mike needs to go to college and be available to look for work and Liam's childcare is still patchy. I thought it might get easier when he went to school, but if we can't find a local school to take him – or one with breakfast clubs or after-school clubs that can cope with him – I don't really see things getting any better.

ACTIVITY 7.4

What class would you say Mike and Clare are in?

Have their cultural values contributed to the difficult situation they are in?

Comment

Sometimes we make value judgements based on knowing only part of a person's story. Without knowing Mike's and Clare's full story there are those who would make value judgements about them that might accuse Mike and Clare of being selfish and lazy for being willing to live on benefit that is provided by the hard work of others. This case study is also an example of how unexpected events happen to everyone and can have a profound effect on a family and their social and financial circumstances.

Many people, from all classes, worry about finding and keeping a job and how they will live once their working life is over. However, those in the working class are more vulnerable to unexpected unemployment particularly where large local employers, such as car manufacturers, close down. They may also be more susceptible to the risk of their skills becoming obsolete as new manufacturing methods are introduced, or the worry that injury may make them unable to work. Living and working with people who share the same concerns as us again leads to a group cultural identity; in such situations it is likely we will develop a similar approach to life and similar strategies to deal with the issues in our environment and may develop strategies which cannot be understood by people not in the same situation.

ACTIVITY 7.5

In achieving the standards for becoming a social worker one of the areas of your professional life you need to reflect on is an awareness of your own values and whether these lead you to hold prejudiced, or unexamined, ideas about the way those you meet live their lives. You are also expected to respect each person as an individual. These can be very challenging things to do, particularly if those we are working with hold very different views to those we hold ourselves. We are not thinking here about more clear-cut situations where the law is there to guide us, but the more day-to-day ways in which we live our lives. What we choose to do with our leisure time, how we spend – or save – our money, the food we choose to eat, etc.

Think about yourself:

- *How do you organise your budget? What are your priorities for spending or saving your money?*

- *What do you do in your leisure time?*

- *How would you describe your approach to buying and preparing food?*

- *What aspects of your life help you to live like this?*

- *Are there any factors that prevent you from making the most of your budget, eating properly or using your leisure time in the best possible way?*

As you read the case study about Kayla below, think about the pressures and priorities Kayla is managing, what judgements are being made about her life and how she should live it. Do you think the advice she is being given is helping her and her children?

CASE STUDY

Kayla has two children, Sammy who is 3 and Shaina who is 5. She is not in contact with the children's father – they split up soon after Sammy was born and have now lost contact. Kayla was encouraged to find a job as she was told it would get her out of the flat, she would begin to get a social life and it would enable her to provide a better standard of living for her children. So Kayla got a job at the local supermarket, working 16 hours a week across three days. On two of the days she starts work at 8.00 a.m. and on the third day she works in the afternoon and finishes at 6.00 p.m.

Kayla says:

> It seemed such a good idea at first, I knew I'd lose some of my benefit money but I thought what I earned would more than make up for that and anyway, I'd be able to buy nice things for Sammy and Shaina and begin to stand on my own two feet. But what's happened? I have to send Sammy to a childminder for all the time I'm at work and Shaina has to be at breakfast club before school on two days a week and at after-school club on Wednesdays. I have to get both children to the childminder at 7.30 a.m. so I can get to work at 8.00 a.m. and the childminder can take Shaina to the breakfast club. The money I get for childcare doesn't cover what

Continued

I need to pay for the children to be looked after and all in all I actually have less money than before I started work. The kids hate it, I'm stressed running from one place to another and then the media and stuff go on about how mums should be at home looking after their children, not going out to work, playing with them so they don't watch too much telly. I'm financially worse off, I'm exhausted and I'm a bad mum.

Comment

Kayla is a good example of someone caught between conflicting values and attitudes that prevail in society. On the one hand there are values and attitudes that pressure her to 'stand on her own feet', to go out to work to support her family and possibly even try to 'better' her family circumstances. However, there are also pressures to be a 'good mum' and stay at home and look after the children. Reflecting on what you have read so far, could you say if these prevailing or dominant values that Kayla is struggling with are working-class values or middle-class values?

The link between low income, poverty and class

We have seen how there have been changes in some of the economic aspects of class in Britain. Indeed, the evidence shows that *the proportion of people in 'middle class' jobs has increased* (Thomson, 2003, p167). However, the number of individuals and families that are living on low incomes or in poverty has actually risen, particularly over the past five years (Poverty Site, 2009).

Poverty is a contentious subject and can be measured in a number of ways. For example, those who are said to be on or below the poverty line can be defined as being unable to buy an agreed notional 'basket of goods' that contains the items necessary for basic standards of food, shelter, clothing, etc. (Hills, 2004, p56). This basket varies and is not the same now as it was in the 1950s when a quarter of British households did not have a bathroom, nor is it the same basket as in, say, a poor rural area in Mexico. The point is that it's relative to the standards of this society now, so assertions about poverty cannot simply be dismissed as not as bad as 'real poverty' in some other country.

Relative poverty can also be measured by income, typically determined as referring to those who earn below the average national income or 60 per cent below the median income. For the year 2006/7 the average income per working person was approximately £24,000 a year, while the median income was £19,600 (possibly a truer representation of how much most people in the UK were living on in 2006/7: Blastland, 2008). The average income is arrived at by adding up all incomes and dividing by the number of people, while the median income is arrived at by lining up all the incomes being measured, lowest to highest, and focusing on the income in the middle. So, while 50 per cent of incomes in 2006/7 were above £19,600, 50 per cent of incomes were below it, remembering also that £19,600 is below the average income of £24,000.

It remains likely that children born into poverty may never escape such circumstances (Preston, 2008). Those who live in poverty are more likely to *experience disability and ill health* (Preston, 2008, p7). Those living in poverty are also more likely to be living in low-quality housing, in cramped conditions with little personal privacy or quiet spaces, and possibly have to move frequently.

Governments have tried different policies to combat poverty but despite many measures poverty still exists in Britain. The competing explanations for this have implications for social work: if people are trapped in poverty despite their best efforts to get out of it there are limits on what you can do to help (and it might affect your attitude, too). If they remain in poverty because they are lazy, have no initiative and live fatalistically only for the present, there may be some intervention you can make (though you might respect them less). The latter explanation for persisting poverty is not one I share, but the belief that those who live in poverty have everything given to them but will not help themselves is held by many, including (probably) many social workers: *negative images of the poor are deeply sedimented, historically* (Jones, 1999, p5).

Actually, cultural attitudes do help to maintain poverty and exclusion, but not always in the way suggested above. Poor people may be very committed to changing their circumstances but be prevented because of the cultural values of others around them, for example owner-occupiers campaigning not to have social housing built near them, or affluent parents using their house-buying power to take all the available places in a good school.

C H A P T E R   S U M M A R Y

This chapter began by stating that class is a challenging term to define. In exploring it we have seen that discussing class includes exploring it as a measurement of economic status and well-being as well as as an expression of personal attitudes, values and beliefs. Discussing class also requires some understanding of how class has been significant historically and why we use the terms working class and middle class to ascribe a class to someone. We have also briefly explored whether there is an implicit assumption that everyone should be striving to be middle class, that it is somehow 'better' to be middle class rather than working class. While we might want to encourage people to aspire to achieve economic well-being in their lives, and we would certainly not want people to be living in poverty, we need to guard against falling into the trap of believing there is only one path to achieving general well-being, particularly if that path is determined by only one class's set of values, attitudes and beliefs. Working with diversity includes understanding and accepting the diversity of values related to class.

FURTHER READING

hooks, b (2000) *Where we stand: Class matters*. Abingdon: Routledge.
bell hooks (whose name is always written in lower case) gives a very accessible, semi-autobiographical account which is a more detailed exploration of many of the issues this chapter has raised. In particular the book is helpful in exploring how contemporary society deals with notions of class and what she sees as the widening gap between rich and poor.

Thomson, K (ed.) (2003) *British social attitudes – the 20th Report: Continuity and change over two decades.* London: Sage.
This explores the values, attitudes and beliefs held by a large cross-section of those who live in Britain. It provides a helpful insight into prevailing attitudes particularly in relation to class (and other inequalities).

Wilkinson, R and Pickett, K (2010) *The spirit level: Why equality is better for everyone.* London: Penguin.
A very readable book by two international experts, comparing societies with relatively narrow economic class differences (like Finland) with societies with bigger gaps (like Britain and the USA). It's easy to dip into, with chapters on teenage births, community life and social relations, and much else.

WEBSITES

www.shelter.org.uk

www.poverty.org.uk

Chapter 8
Race and ethnicity

Vini Lander

Introduction

The ongoing debate related to race and ethnicity is complex and multidimensional. The media headlines, political interventions and soundbites can serve to cloud the debate as well as add, at times, spurious dimensions to discussions about race and ethnicity. This chapter requires the reader to establish for themselves an understanding of their own identity in order to appreciate their position regarding this debate and to understand how their position may shape their responses to others (see Activity 8.1). The terms race and ethnicity can evoke a variety of responses from different people which are often based on their positive or negative experiences of issues related to these terms. The whole area of race and ethnicity is perceived by some as controversial or one which promotes controversy and some people prefer to steer clear of it. In doing so they adopt one of two recognisable stances: either polite and seemingly compliant silence or vociferous denial and defence.

ACTIVITY *8.1*

What was your initial reaction to this chapter heading? On a piece of paper, which you can refer to later, write down five words to describe yourself.

This chapter aims to explore the meaning of the terms race, ethnicity and racism in order to establish a baseline of understanding on which subsequent discussion in this chapter will be based and that activities will draw on. The chapter will examine the nature of Britain as a multicultural society and how legislation informs our responses within a professional context. This will then be contrasted with how the perpetuation of stereotypes, myths about political correctness, misguided or confused 'colour blindness', or even a liberal or our own personal position can inform our responses to issues of race, culture and ethnicity. It is important to acknowledge that working within a caring profession such as social work and tackling issues of inequality, whether they are related to race and ethnicity or another dimension, can be quite challenging on a personal and institutional level. It is important that you start your journey and that you are able to acknowledge that you have travelled some way already, while acknowledging there are still uncharted miles ahead. Clearly, being committed to the journey is an important aspect of your personal and professional development within this profession.

Multicultural Britain – a short historical overview

In professional and academic literature and in our daily lives most people accept that Britain is a multicultural and multilingual society. Some people mistakenly think that in historical terms this is a relatively recent phenomenon arising from the arrival of the first Black immigrants from the Caribbean on the *Empire Windrush* in 1948, or the arrival of people from the Indian subcontinent not long afterwards, both at the invitation of the British government to address the labour shortage at the time, or even with the arrival of

Ugandan Asians expelled by Idi Amin in 1973. However, Britain was and had been a multi-cultural country long before the 1950s. There were Black soldiers who accompanied the Roman army and later became slaves; Jewish settlement in this country dates from 1066; Muslim sailors came to Britain as part of the crews of merchant ships in the eighteenth century. In fact, historical documents acknowledge the presence of Black people in Britain since the sixteenth century.

The arrival of a significant number of people from different cultures sparked the debates about how the country they came to responded to their presence. In addition to the racist attitudes that were revealed there were debates about whether these new immigrants should be assimilated into mainstream culture, in other words whether they should melt into mainstream white British society by dropping their own cultural and religious beliefs in an attempt to follow the old adage 'when in Rome do as the Romans do'. An alternative more pluralistic response suggested society should acknowledge the differences that these incoming groups brought and permit such differences to exist alongside mainstream culture. The debate today has moved on to examine how the notion of Britishness can be developed *within* a pluralist multicultural society.

Another popular misconception is that Britain is being overrun by immigrants or Black people (sometimes these are assumed to be the same, sometimes not). At the last census 8 per cent of the population belonged to a minority ethnic group. Of course, there are areas of the country where the population of those from minority ethnic groups is more concentrated and this may give rise to the misconception that there are more people from these groups in the country. See the interactive maps on www.multiverse.ac.uk to find out the makeup of the population within your county.

CASE STUDY

A Bangladeshi family

Mohammed Aslam is a 14-year-old boy who lives with his 12-year-old sister and his newly widowed mother in a block of flats in an inner city. The school educational welfare officer (EWO) has noted that neither Mohammed nor his sister Abida Begum have been attending school regularly. He has visited their home but found that the mother could not speak English and the children's English was insufficiently developed to provide explanations for their school absences. He returns with a colleague who speaks Sylheti. She finds out that the mother and children had only been in the country for six months when the father (who was older than the children's mother) suffered a heart attack and died. They have no immediate family in the city and an uncle 60 miles away has done a little to support the family. Mohammed has felt the burden of responsibility to protect his mother against the racist violence and bullying they have suffered from their neighbour upstairs. She has thrown down rubbish, excrement and other things onto their balcony; her children have persistently rung the doorbell at all times and when Mohammed and Abida have tried to go to school on their mother's insistence they have been the victims of spitting, name calling and jostling on their way to and at the bus stop.

You have been contacted by the EWO. How will you help and support this family?

Understanding terminology

The purpose of this section is not to provide a comprehensive guide on the use of terms but to provide a basic foundation for the beginning professional. It is important that as professionals in a caring profession we do not shy away from using terms such as Black or Asian, Indian, etc. to refer to clients' ethnicity. Their ethnicity is an important aspect of their identity and may be a key consideration in how you deal with their case. Depending on your own exposure to racial and cultural diversity you may not feel comfortable or able to use such terms. Your level of comfort may be dependent not only on whether you have met and engaged with people from different ethnic groups, but may be affected by your own position, the media coverage of race issues or just lack of information and understanding. Many people avoid engaging in conversations or discussions about race because they feel they are unable to use the right terms and feel that they are 'treading on eggshells' for fear of using the wrong term and afraid of inadvertently upsetting someone from a minority ethnic group through their inappropriate use of language. While this is an important consideration, nevertheless, we all have a duty within a racially, culturally and linguistically diverse society to become (multi)culturally literate.

The word race (or as it is often written 'race') has no biological basis but is a socially constructed term. We are one race or species, namely *homo sapiens*. However, the term race is still used to categorise humans with different observable characteristics such as skin colour, hair colour/texture and facial features. The term is used socially to delineate groups of people with similar physical characteristics. The classification of people into different races has its roots in Victorian scientists' attempts to discover and order the natural world; they tried to link visible features of groups of people to their cultural characteristics and used one to explain the other. Although Timbuktu's main trade in the 1500s was in books and the remarkable artistic heritage of the kingdom of Benin is now recognised, African non-industrial societies were seen through European eyes at the time as primitive and less capable of becoming civilised; it was therefore acceptable to enslave them. Such classification ensured that ideas about the inferiority of Black people and the superiority of the White coloniser became embedded within European societies, who were all either engaged in colonisation or benefitting from it.

However, the classification of individuals can vary according to the society they live in. For example, in apartheid South Africa a hierarchical structure was constructed on racial ascriptions as defined by the ruling White group. There were separate and inferior amenities for Black people and those classified as 'coloured' (i.e. mixed). In the USA, blackness was associated with slavery for two centuries, and post-slavery the term 'coloured' came to be seen as more polite than 'black'. This has been less and less so for the past 50 years, and indeed referring to an African American as 'coloured' today is likely to produce an angry reaction from a people who want to assert there is nothing shameful about their skin colour. This lesson has not yet been learned in Britain, with many White people feeling it is better to use the term 'coloured' instead of referring to a person as Indian or Black. In my view, 'coloured' carries with it connotations of inferiority rather than affirmation of identity and cultural heritage, and I would much rather someone referred to me as Indian than called me coloured. Indeed Gaine (2005, p91) argues *White people should never use the term, especially if they are more comfortable with it*, so if you are more comfortable with it, it's worth thinking about why.

The term ethnic group refers to a group of people who are distinguished by their customs, heritage, language or religion, so these kinds of things make up their ethnicity. We all belong to an ethnic group and have ethnicity. The term 'ethnic' seems to have taken on another meaning in terms of everyday usage. For example, certain fashion trends will be described as ethnic to denote Indian, Asian or African influences or merely to indicate that they are non-mainstream and slightly exotic. There is also confusion about how to use the terms ethnic minority or minority ethnic to describe people from African, Caribbean, Asian or Chinese backgrounds. As Gillborn (1990, p5) notes the term ethnic minority *is usually taken to imply minority status not only in numerical terms, but also in power terms*, hence it is better to refer to people who are from a minority group as Black and minority ethnic or BME. It is seen by some as an affirming term which identifies a group who are collectively subject to racism. In the past this has most often been as a result of their skin colour, though not always, as in the case of Jews. As the population of Britain changes as a result of European migrant workers entering and settling in the UK, the abbreviation BME often now includes them too, though we have to be aware that this terminology may change.

Although race may be a social construct in the present day and throughout history the effects of racism have been all too visible and tangible. Racism is the act of discriminating, advantaging or disadvantaging people based on their colour, ethnic origin or culture (Macpherson, 1999). In order to advantage or disadvantage a person or a group you have to have power to exercise and establish your actions. In most cases it is those who are in the majority that can exercise such power and follow through discriminatory or racist assumptions, though an exception to this was the concentration of power in the White minority in South Africa. In Britain and the United States it is the White majority that holds power and as such racism is often associated as an issue related to White–Black populations. Gillborn (1990, p8) stresses that it is power plus prejudice which results in racism: it is the structural power of the majority which results in racism.

The notion of racism has been further extended and nowadays people refer to racisms to encompass a range of exclusionary attitudes or detrimental outcomes for some people. It encompasses old-fashioned 'racism, xenophobia and anti-Semitism', recognising that discrimination and hatred are not just dependent on physical appearance but that they can arise as a result of language, culture and religion (Parekh, 2000), as recently evidenced by the growing demonisation of Muslims and referred to as Islamophobia. Cultural racism refers to the way in which minority cultures are thought of as inferior or deficient in some way when compared to the majority culture which is thought to be the norm. This sort of stance can lead to the devaluing of other cultures and the privileging of mainstream culture which is used as a benchmark by which other cultures are judged.

The term 'institutional racism' came into common parlance as a result of the Macpherson Report in 1999 following the inquiry into the death of Stephen Lawrence. The Report defined it as follows.

> *The collective failure of an organisation to provide an appropriate and professional service to people because of their colour, culture, or ethnic origin. It can be seen or detected in processes, attitudes and behaviour which amount to discrimination through unwitting prejudice, ignorance, thoughtlessness and racist stereotyping which disadvantage minority ethnic people.*
>
> (Para. 6.34, www.archive.official-documents.co.uk)

While this was the definition drawn up and used by the Inquiry it is interesting to note that the paragraph which followed the definition, as shown below, clearly outlines how it comes into existence within an organisation and how it can 'wear away' or corrode institutions. It implicitly indicates that racism within an institution is the responsibility of all within it.

> *It persists because of the failure of the organisation openly and adequately to recognise and address its existence and causes by policy, example and leadership. Without recognition and action to eliminate such racism it can prevail as part of the ethos or culture of the organisation. It is a corrosive disease.*
>
> (Para. 6.34, www.archive.official-documents.co.uk)

Many people disputed and still contest that institutional racism exists. This is due to two reasons. First, institutional racism is not apparent in overtly racist language or actions. It is invisible but nevertheless tangible in other ways such as in recruitment, retention, progression and achievement of BME people or employees within an institution and the services it should provide. Secondly, because it seems to be hidden it is harder to identify and easier to deny.

Ryde (2009) stresses that we live in a society which has deeply held ideas about race and as such describes society as racialised. Her research focuses on looking at the position of being a white professional who did not think that she belonged to a 'race' and how the maintenance of this position *perpetuates the racialisation of society and, in particular, the professions within it* (Ryde, 2009, p15).

Race and the law

There has been a series of Race Relations Acts since the first in 1965 and 1968. The latter made it unlawful to refuse housing, schooling or employment on the grounds of a person's race, colour or ethnicity. This Act was replaced by the Race Relations Act in 1976 which extended the areas to which the Act applied, identified direct and indirect racism and established the Commission for Racial Equality. This Act was then amended following, but not as a result of, the Macpherson Inquiry in 1999. The Race Relations Amendment Act 2000 introduced a different dimension to the legislation: the requirement to be proactive in the pursuit for equal opportunities and good race relations. The Act placed a statutory duty on public authorities to have due regard to the need:

- to eliminate unlawful racial discrimination;

- to promote equality of opportunity and good relations between persons of different racial groups.

(www.opsi.gov.uk/acts)

This implies that public bodies needed to monitor their recruitment, provision and delivery of services with respect to meeting the needs of all groups within society. Hence the monitoring and benchmarks identified by many local authorities regarding recruitment and retention targets for staff but also the setting of service targets. The race relations legislation and the equality duty cover another and probably the most marginalised people in the UK, Gypsy, Roma and Traveller groups. In research commissioned by the Equalities and Human Rights Commission (2009) the report notes:

> One core theme which arises across all topics is the pervasive and corrosive impact of experiencing racism and discrimination throughout an entire lifespan and in employment, social and public contexts. Existing evidence, including from the consultation, highlights high rates of anxiety, depression and at times self-destructive behaviour (for example, suicide and/or substance abuse). These are, on the face of the evidence, responses to 'cultural trauma' produced by the failings of 21st century British society and public bodies' failure to engage in an equitable manner with members of the communities. Having reviewed the strength of the evidence of the prejudice and discrimination faced by Gypsies and Travellers, the authors of the report were surprised that more members of the Gypsy and Traveller communities had not succumbed to negativity, and remained resilient in the face of what are often multiple and complex forms of exclusion.

> (www.equalityhumanrights.com)

In 2003 another set of regulations governed the discrimination that some had suffered due to their religion. The Employment Equality (Religion and Beliefs) Regulations 2003 made it illegal to discriminate against someone on the basis of their religion or beliefs (Jews and Sikhs were already protected as ethnic groups under the race relations legislation). These regulations came about due to growing Islamophobia, even before the 9/11 and 7/7 incidents.

In your everyday working life as a social worker you may not consciously be aware of the race relations legislation or even have to think about it until you get a case similar to the one below. Think through how you would respond and note the steps that would form your actions regarding the phone call.

ACTIVITY 8.2

An irate relative has just phoned you about one of your elderly clients. They are enraged that their mother is being cared for by

> ... one of those Polish immigrants who does not even speak English properly so how can she see to the needs of my mother? My mother does not understand anything this carer is saying. What are social services doing employing people who come to this country and who cannot speak the language to look after the vulnerable elderly?

Comment

This will tax your skills in listening to service users on the one hand and not condoning prejudice and discrimination on the other. It may be that the Polish care worker does speak reasonable English and that the (possible) confusion of an older service user and the extreme anxiety of a worried relative have combined into an angry and unreasonable rejection of the worker. It's also possible that the provider (not the social services department directly) has employed someone without the level of English fluency required for the work. Either way, you will have to find out more about the care worker, probably by meeting her, and you'll have to listen to and support the carer and his/her mother without any suggestion that they can reject a care worker on nationality grounds alone. The fact is a lot of care work at various levels from cleaning to nursing is done by foreign nationals, and at lower wage rates than most British staff would be prepared to accept.

RESEARCH SUMMARY

Gypsy and Roma Travellers

The Equality and Human Rights Commission Research Report 12 entitled Inequalities experienced by Gypsy and Traveller communities: A review *(Cemlyn, et al., 2009) outlines research related to the area of social work and social provision for Gypsies and Travellers. It notes that this is a more vulnerable group due to the levels of inequalities they suffer across a range of services which are also covered in the report. There is little quantitative data related to this group due to the lack of ethnic monitoring related to Gypsy and Traveller people living on sites. It notes evidence that there is a lack of trust between social services and Gypsies and Travellers, particularly in the case of Irish, Romany and New Travellers. There is a fear that their children will be taken away, a fear related to real policies in the past that involved educating young children away from their culture. The report acknowledges that this fear was mirrored in the ignorance and misunderstanding of Gypsy and Traveller cultures demonstrated by social workers and it outlines a number of cases of discrimination and institutionally racist practice. For example:*

> A case study of young homeless Irish Travellers found that social services' response to a child protection referral from a voluntary agency took no account of the young people's situation and only offered engagement on the department's own terms, what the author referred to as 'institutional blindness' ... Garrett ... found strong evidence of racism towards Irish Travellers, which 'appears to combine a culturally embedded anti-Irish racism with a more pervasive antipathy towards the unsettled, strangers and migrant populations' ... Instances were cited where social workers explicitly advocated the 'breaking' of Traveller culture.
>
> (Cemlyn, et al., 2009, pp129–30)

The report concludes that while many social workers undertake training in anti-oppressive practice, aspects of this training fail to feature in social workers' responses and consideration of cases involving Gypsy and Traveller communities. Its final and fourteenth recommendation states:

> A human rights approach needs to be further developed in social work theory and practice alongside existing approaches that promote equality practice.
>
> (Cemlyn, et al., 2009, p148)

ACTIVITY *8.3*

Read pp125–48 of this report and outline implications for your training (find it at www. equalityhumanrights.com and put 'gypsy traveller' into the search box). How much of your training has related to understanding and meeting the needs of Gypsy, Roma and Traveller people? What do you need to research/find out about these communities? What shifts in attitude/perceptions do you need to make in relation to Gypsies, Roma and Travellers who may live in the area you are training or working in?

Understanding our position as professionals

ACTIVITY *8.4*

Now return to that piece of paper where you used five words to describe yourself. Do any of the words refer to your gender, to your ethnicity or racial group, linguistic heritage or culture or religion? If any of these aspects featured in your description of yourself ask why this might be. If not, why did they not feature on your list?

I would describe myself as a British-Sikh female. I associate myself more with my religion than my Asian/Indian heritage since I was not born in India or in Britain. When I conduct a similar exercise with my students it is interesting to note that many from minority ethnic backgrounds mention their own ethnicity, but those who could be described as White British rarely mention theirs. Why do you think that is?

Comment

The next section asks you to explore your own position and what you bring to your chosen career in terms of your own identity, cultural beliefs and values. Some people may find this section quite challenging while others may read it and get the overall point, but may need to reread it in order to fully understand the implications of it within the process of becoming a social worker. Whatever your responses to this section make a note of them then ask yourself why you responded in this way. Judy Ryde (2009, p24) writes about her responses and subsequent reflections on them with reference to working with Black clients. She cites an example of a Black African client in a counselling session who chose to sit on the floor. She reflects on her responses to this, such as perhaps he is not used to chairs evoking the notion of him being primitive. She urges us not to jump to a 'politically correct' response but to allow ourselves to be aware of these unconscious assumptions and why they are there.

In exploring the persistence of racism within society and institutions writers such as King (2004) describe a racism which is 'dysconscious' which she implies is almost embedded so deep within the person's psyche that they are unaware of it. She describes it as

> ... a form of racism that tacitly accepts White norms and privileges. It is the absence of consciousness (i.e. not unconscious) but an impaired consciousness.

> (King, 2004, p73)

Other writers such as Grover (1997) argue that someone growing up as a White person never has to think about it and is not reminded of it: it is transparent or invisible and seen as a neutral position. The current emergent thinking informed by debates in the USA examines the notion of Whiteness as a position which is occupied by the majority; it is one of privilege. Marx (2006) describes Whiteness as not just racial performance which replicates privilege embedded in institutional power but encompassing qualities such as *cultures, histories, experiences, discourses and privileges shared by Whites* (2006, p6). She associates the notion of Whiteness with a commonly held position described as colour-blindness where the person maintains that they do not recognise or see the colour or culture of a person, that to them the other person is a person and by the mere virtue of exercising a colour-blind position equity is established. This is a stance maintained by many who would consider themselves as liberal and open-minded and not at all racist.

Such a position in studying the responses of trainee teachers to the presence of minority ethnic children in their class is questioned by R Jones (1999). He noted how the student teachers would ignore the ethnicity of these children and would take no account of their ethnicity or background within their daily practice; he termed this oversight making the children 'white by proxy'. He thought this happened because the teachers wanted to adopt a liberal colour-blind position. He also postulated that in some way they may have associated skin colour, minority ethnicity or race with a deficit model of thinking whereby professionals feel that some kind of compensatory action needs to be taken with people from Black and minority ethnic (BME) groups.

ACTIVITY *8.5*

List your own thoughts about the liberal White position. Does it advantage White people or not? Justify your answer with reference to theory, research observations and practice.

McIntosh (1990) delineates 25 privileges associated with being White which she likens to being carried in an invisible knapsack. She writes that in listing such advantages she felt she could no longer hold on to the notion of meritocracy.

What do you understand by the term meritocracy? (See glossary.) How and why does McIntosh feel that for her as a White woman who has listed how her own ethnicity affords her many advantages her notion of meritocracy is compromised?

Comment

If you're White and British, it can be hard to look this topic in the eye and not feel you're being accused of something (and thus get defensive). The opening chapter of this book asserts that everyone has prejudices; this chapter is not implying that in some way Black people are nicer or more humane than Whites. You're being asked here to look at things about race and ethnicity you might take for granted, that may be invisible to you, but may be all too visible to someone with a BME background. If comparisons help, female readers might consider how males have a completely different experience on public transport at night (and may not realise it); someone with good hearing might think how often they have been utterly excluded by a quiet mumbled delivery in a seminar; LGB readers will know about routine assumptions that everyone is heterosexual. These are other forms of invisible knapsacks.

The study of Whiteness has arisen from the need to understand how racism and disadvantage have not been defeated. If disadvantage exists for some groups then it follows that advantage must also exist for others. Pearce (2005, p133) writes about the important need to understand one's own position of being White, in her case as a teacher in a multi-ethnic school, in order to tackle issues of racism and understand its functioning within an institutional setting:

> ... because Whiteness is rarely acknowledged as a racial identity, that process is likely to be more difficult for White teachers – and is all the more vital for that.

Ryde (2009, p37) summarises the issue by noting that White people do not recognise or acknowledge that in social terms they have a race and assume that race is a problem associated with others who do, namely those from minority ethnic groups.

ACTIVITY **8.6**

You have just overheard the conversation below taking place between two student social work colleagues.

Sophie: I don't know why they always bang on about race and racial issues. I am mixed race and I've never had a problem with it. Isn't it about time that we moved on and treated people as people rather than a colour?

Gary: I didn't know you were mixed race ... I mean it doesn't show. I think it is important to talk about it. Look at me, I have only ever known White middle-class suburbia and schools and now I am at Hamchester University and there still aren't any here. If I work in London I'm going to struggle, aren't I?

Sophie: Why should you? Like I said, they are people, just treat them like people. It's just making it all very complicated. You won't know about every religion and things if you do work in London, so it's best to treat them like I said, just as people.

Gary: I know I am not going to know about every religion and that, but it is a bit more complex than treating people as people, isn't it?

Sophie: Not if you ask me. I think it is just what my mum says, political correctness gone mad. Just tell them what they want to hear in the essay and then just do what I just said, treat them like people.

Can you analyse this conversation in terms of the position of each student and then your own? What are the implicit or hidden assumptions?

Comment

Political correctness is a term which has been misappropriated by the Right to ridicule attempts to raise people's awareness and consciousness about issues related to equality. It is also a notion bandied about by others who want to avoid addressing issues of inherent inequality and indeed is now usually used in a derogatory way to highlight how practices and language allegedly serve to advantage minorities at the expense of the White majority. The examples they give are frequently exaggerated or even mythical. The term 'political correctness' was in fact a response by left-wing American academics who were gently mocking their own efforts to ensure that their language and actions were respectful and reflective in relation to minority groups (www.multiverse.ac.uk). All too often in the press there are exclamations of 'political correctness gone mad' and, depending on your own understanding of the issues and your own position, you may be able to see beyond such headlines. They merely serve to detract from the real task at hand within our society, namely the elimination of racism and inequality. In other words, mythology about PC is a smokescreen to avoid the real work of establishing equality. Gaine (2005, p88) stresses that this mythology has played on the uncertainty, ignorance and some unwillingness to offend of many white British people. The problem is not the attempt to avoid language that routinely insults people; it's in the mocking reaction of those too complacent to think about it seriously.

CASE STUDY

Sardar* Harbhajan Singh Gill

Sardar Harbhajan Singh Gill lives with his son, daughter-in-law and two granddaughters in a leafy Buckinghamshire town. He moved to the UK about 30 years ago after having run a successful transport business in Nairobi, Kenya. He was a successful businessman but the political climate in Kenya was such that he felt he had to get his family out to live in a safer environment. He had many relatives already residing in the UK.

He is 77 years old and lost his wife two years ago. Ever since her death his own mental condition has deteriorated. He has gone out for walks and got lost, not knowing how to get back home. His memories of the past are strong and he can still converse in Swahili (not his mother tongue, which is Punjabi) which he used extensively in business in Nairobi. In fact he speaks five languages including English. Both his son and daughter-in-law work and the children go to school. He spends his day alone at home; there are very few Sikh or other Indian or minority ethnic families in the area. In his isolation he gets confused, he is lonely and he forgets a lot. His family have become concerned about his condition and sought advice from their GP, but the information gained was limited. They have now phoned the local social services in an attempt to get some advice on how to help and support their elderly relative.

How would you advise this family? What can they do to help Sardar Harbhajan Singh Gill? Is there any additional information that you require?

*(*Sardar literally means 'leader' but tends to be used instead of Mr within the Punjabi Indian/Pakistani community, particularly for an elderly man.)*

Asylum seekers

In March 2009 Refugee and Migrant Justice published a report entitled Does every child matter? Children seeking asylum in Britain. It aimed to examine the government commitment to keep children seeking asylum safe and to apply the same principles to their safety as afforded to children who are British citizens. The code issued by the government is found in the UK Border Agency's Code of Practice for Keeping Children Safe from Harm published in January 2009. The report outlines that of the 7,000 or so children who enter the asylum-seeking process approximately 3,500 are unaccompanied children, some of whom have been trafficked into the country. The report shows that the government falls short in its commitment to protect such vulnerable children who at times are seeking asylum from war-torn regions of the world such as Iraq or Afghanistan. In some cases they may be with their families or some members of their families; in other cases they are lone, unaccompanied children who are likely to be traumatised by their experiences in their home country as well as the abuse they have suffered at the hands of adults involved in their transit across various countries. The report notes:

> Almost half of the unaccompanied children who arrived here had experienced combat in their home country and nearly 40% had witnessed or experienced torture. Many are suffering from post-traumatic stress.

> (Refugee and Migrant Justice, 2009, p3)

You are advised to read the full report and then respond to the questions raised after reading the following case study which is taken from the report.

A failed asylum seeker

Client C, arrived in the UK in 2007 when she was 12 (her age is in dispute and the UK Border Agency are currently treating her as being two years older). Her claim is based on ethnic violence in her country. Among other things, she witnessed the murder of her father. She fled to a neighbouring country where she was befriended by a man who offered to look after her. The man arranged for her to travel to the UK. After her arrival, the man took her to a house where, after several days, he forced her to have sex with him and another man. She managed to escape from the house and soon after came into contact with social services who took her into care. She discovered she was pregnant and had a termination. She was 13 at the time. She was interviewed about her claim for asylum a year ago and refused asylum earlier this year, the UK Border Agency rejecting her claim in its entirety as well as her account of how she came to the UK. Although it has a letter from the Metropolitan Police confirming that it is investigating the matter, the Agency did not believe she had been trafficked to the UK. The decision makes only one reference to her pregnancy, referring to her termination, but noting she was now in good health.

Continued

It does not appear to have occurred to the UK Border Agency that the pregnancy may be evidence of trafficking of the most abusive kind. (Refugee and Migrant Justice, 2009, p9).

As the social worker involved in this case, what legal and social knowledge and understanding do you need to be aware of and to support Client C? While the process of creating a case for asylum is the remit of a solicitor, in your role as her assigned social worker how can you support and help this girl?

C H A P T E R   S U M M A R Y

What you do matters

This chapter has outlined a number of key issues related to racial, cultural and linguistic diversity. It has provided an overview of some key aspects of the debate which all social workers should be conversant with, for example the associated terminology and legislation. The chapter has also sought to challenge current thinking about race issues to examine why it is still not 'sorted' yet. In an attempt to illuminate this area the reader has been challenged to examine their own position with reference to race issues. Social workers are professionals who attempt, and work, to alleviate the outcomes of inequality or inequitable systems, so social workers are inextricably linked to the achievement of social justice and a more equal society. One chapter alone cannot improve practice in race equality in social work – it is only the continued commitment and endeavour of individuals which will make a difference in the lives of all people using social services.

FURTHER READING

Parekh, B (2000) *The future of multi-ethnic Britain*. London: Profile Books.

This is a really comprehensive and thoughtful review of all aspects of racial and ethnic relations, clearly set out, with many stimulating ideas.

WEBSITES

www.multiverse.ac.uk
Though this is designed for student teachers, it contains a wealth of information, from statistical details by area to research reports to conference summaries.

www.britkid.org
This was originally written for secondary schools but its clear and graphic format makes it a very accessible source for key ideas presented briefly.

www.runnymedetrust.org
This is the leading race and ethnicity think tank/research organisation/policy pressure group. It has a constantly renewed stock of recent reports on everything from specific ethnic groups to financial exclusion.

Chapter 9
Faith and religion

Chris Gaine

A C H I E V I N G   A   S O C I A L   W O R K   D E G R E E

This chapter will help you meet the following National Occupational Standards.

Key Role 1: Prepare for, and work with individuals, families, carers, groups and communities to assess their needs and circumstances.

- Prepare for social work contact and involvement.
- Work with individuals, families, carers, groups and communities to help them make informed decisions.

Key Role 2: Plan, carry out, review and evaluate social work practice, with individuals, families, carers, groups, communities and other professionals.

- Interact with individuals, families, carers, groups and communities to achieve change and development and to improve life opportunities.

Key Role 3: Support individuals to represent their needs, views and circumstances.

- Advocate with, and on behalf of, individuals, families, carers, groups and communities.

Key Role 6: Demonstrate professional competence in social work practice.

- Research, analyse, evaluate and use current knowledge of best social work practice.

It will also introduce you to the following academic standards as set out in the social work subject benchmark statement.

5.1.1 Social work services, service users and carers.

- Explanations of the links between definitional processes contributing to social differences (for example, social class, gender, ethnic differences, age, sexuality and religious belief) to the problems of inequality and differential need faced by service users.
- The nature of social work services in a diverse society (with particular reference to concepts such as prejudice, interpersonal, institutional and structural discrimination, empowerment and anti-discriminatory practices).

5.1.3 Values and ethics.

- The moral concepts of rights, responsibility, freedom, authority and power inherent in the practice of social workers as moral and statutory agents.

5.5.3 Analysis and synthesis.

- Assess the merits of contrasting theories, explanations, research, policies and procedures.
- Critically analyse and take account of the impact of inequality and discrimination in work with people in particular contexts and problem situations.

Introduction

We live in contradictory times with regard to religion. On the one hand religious observance among the majority of the population is lower than it has ever been, especially among Anglicans (also known as the Church of England), historically the largest branch of Christianity in Britain: less than a million Anglicans attend church weekly. In other words, Britain is much more secular than it used to be. On the other hand, religious observance measured by attendance at worship is strongest among those with immigrant roots: Irish and Polish Catholics, Caribbean and African Christians of various kinds, Muslims, Sikhs and Hindus. In complex ways, therefore, religion in Britain has connections with race and ethnicity.

There are other sociological details worth reminding ourselves about, mostly showing the importance of Christianity in the past and how this lives on in British institutions. The Anglican Church has special status, with all its English bishops having seats in the House of Lords, the Sovereign at its head and considerable formal involvement in schooling. While its active membership is declining here, the majority of Anglicans in the world live in Africa and this has implications for various social issues because a substantial proportion of African bishops are more traditional in their views about marriage, homosexuality, abortion and women clergy than their British counterparts, so the senior archbishops are constantly brokering compromises. When giving evidence in court the expectation is that people will swear an oath on their holy book (usually the Bible) and one has to ask specially to deviate from this. Christianity also plays a part in all state occasions – coronations, acts of remembrance, the opening of Parliament, prayers in wartime – and it remains the default setting for funerals and cremations (though most children are no longer baptised and only about a third of marriages take place in churches: ONS, 2007).

A peculiarity in this increasingly secular society is that for decades we had northern Europe's most intractable civil conflict with at least a partly-religious basis, in Northern Ireland, resulting in thousands of killings over a forty-year period. There was more to it than religion, but nevertheless two different forms of Christianity were often invoked as a justification for social divisions (and still are: Hughes, 2009). Northern Ireland had a law against religious discrimination in employment long before the rest of the UK, and still has differences in abortion law and the age of consent for gay sex.

A final element of faith in Britain today that is worth mentioning is the rise in what are commonly called 'new age' beliefs: a range of spiritual ideas too wide to be detailed here, containing many beliefs often reformulated from other times or other places, such as paganism, Scientology and the Hare Krishna movement. It is hard to know the total percentage of the population following such beliefs, especially the very broad range of ideas and practices that might be called 'spiritual'.

I called the above brief survey contradictory. One consequence is that it makes life as a social worker unpredictable. We are living in a time of religious decline, but not entirely.

Definitions and terminology

At this point it is as well to be clear about terminology. Given the importance of religion to some people it is easy to cause offence by referring to things inappropriately. Bearing in mind that most British people – including presumably most social workers – are not active churchgoers, you may be unfamiliar with some of the terminology used already. Later in this chapter there is a detailed chart summarising key differences (and similarities) between the main faiths represented in Britain, but for the moment here is a brief glossary of some key terms.

Bishop A senior person in either the Catholic or Anglican Church, usually responsible for a geographical area (diocese). Archbishops are higher and there are fewer of them; the Catholic Church has just one special archbishop for the whole of Britain: a cardinal (while the head of the Catholic Church worldwide is, of course, the Pope).

Evangelical Seeking to convert others to the faith, especially in Christianity. Proselytising means pretty much the same thing for any faith.

Fundamentalist Someone who holds to certain fundamental beliefs, usually taken literally from their holy book, which are not negotiable or subject to change. All religions have some followers who are fundamentalists and a majority who are not, and it is a mistake to regard the word as somehow synonymous with Muslims.

Islamic Relating to the Muslim faith.

Islamist Claiming to relate to the Islamic faith, but the word is often used to refer to those supporting terrorism in the name of Islam, thus distinguishing between them and other Muslims.

Orthodox Claiming to be the right or correct or most authentic interpretation of religious texts or teachings (though the claim may be disputed by others). Also the name of the third main branch of Christianity, after Catholicism and Protestantism.

Protestant and Roman Catholic The two main divisions within British Christianity. Anglicans are the largest group of Protestants, but there are a great many 'free' Protestant churches (so called because they do not have a relationship with the state) such as Methodist, Presbyterian, Baptist, Congregationalist, Salvation Army, Unitarian, Church of Scotland and Pentecostalist.

Sect A group following a very specific set of beliefs. The word is often used by existing authorities in a faith to distance themselves from a newer sub-group with different inter-pretations. It is seldom used by any group about themselves.

Secular Non-religious (so Register Office weddings are secular, and there are organisa-tions that help organise secular funerals).

Preconceptions

It is difficult not to have preconceptions about people with religious faith, but it is worth considering what these are based upon. Inevitably every reader of this book will have had contact with Christians, whether openly declared as such or not. Fewer will have knowingly had personal or professional contact with people from other faiths and indeed, given the concentration of ethnic minorities in parts of some urban areas, many people, including trainee social workers, are unlikely to have discussed any aspect of religion with a Sikh, Jew, Hindu, Buddhist or – most significantly – a Muslim.

ACTIVITY 9.1

Consider the previous paragraph and list the people you know or have known in the past who belong to different faiths. Were particular aspects of their behaviour or their relationship with you affected by their beliefs? (The answer is relevant either way.) Do you have any way of knowing how typical they were of their faith group?

Comment

When dealing with a client of a religious faith you're not familiar with, some research will be needed. If you look again at the standards cited at the beginning of this chapter you will see several that require sensitive and informed recognition of perspectives that may be different from your own. Later in this chapter is a chart that summarises key features of the world's largest faiths.

I suggested above that Muslims are more significant because of the image of Muslims and of Islam. Contrasting ways of viewing Islam are summed up in Table 9.1.

Table 9.1 Summary of contrasting ways of viewing Islam

Closed, prejudiced view of Islam	Open, unprejudiced view of Islam
Islam is seen as ...	Islam is seen as ...
• the same everywhere, unchanging, unbending	• varying in different places, with Muslims debating changes and having different views
• having no ideas and values in common with other faiths, and no links with them	• having some shared ideas with other faiths and aims and valuing communication
• inferior to Europe and the USA, barbaric, primitive, sexist	• different but not inferior to Western world views and worthy of respect
• violent, aggressive, threatening	• peaceful and maybe a partner in co-operating and solving shared problems
• not European	• having a long history within Europe with an influence in science and architecture
• not belonging in Britain	• the faith of many British, French and German people, so is here to stay
• always unfairly critical of 'the West'	• perhaps having a view on life and the world worth listening to
• too strict, especially on girls and young people	• having strong moral standards

Adapted from www.britkid.org.

We live in a time when religion is more significant on the national and world stage than it has been (arguably) for centuries because of the engagement of Islam in world politics. That, you may realise, is a careful choice of words. Others would cite the threat of terrorism in the name of Islam (Islamist) as something that has affected many aspects of everyday life where large numbers are vulnerable to attack (aeroplanes, theatres, many public buildings, all state buildings) and there is a widespread assumption that Muslims are to be feared, must not be offended, are all fundamentalists and so on. This is explored in Table 9.1 and there is not the space here to expand upon it in detail, but there are two common processes at work in any faith group that need to be understood: first, the variations in belief within faith groups; and second, the blurring between religious teaching per se and everyday cultural practices.

For outsiders to any faith these are difficult to disentangle. How is a Sikh to know where the cultural (or indeed commercial) festival of Christmas ends and the religious significance begins? Would anyone expect a Hindu to realise that while Santa Claus may have some historical basis in St Nicholas, his mythical form with reindeer and presents has nothing whatever to do with Christianity? How easy would it be for many of those who write 'Christian' on a hospital admissions form to explain to a Jew why some Christians believe the Biblical account of the earth being created in seven days is literally true, while others believe it is simply a metaphor? How many could explain why a Protestant leader in Northern Ireland said to a large public gathering that the recent death of a Pope was a cause for them to celebrate?

In the same vein, it is worth addressing some common misconceptions for those less familiar with non-Christian faiths: arranged marriages are decreed by none of them; forced marriage might be justified by those doing the forcing on the grounds of obedience to parents but this is a cultural interpretation, not something laid down in scripture; the same must be said for so-called 'honour killings'. The position of women is ambiguous (to put it mildly) in all world faiths and in general the inequality that's often evident is more a feature of culture than theology (Mumtaz and Shaheed, 1987). Last, female genital mutilation has no basis whatever in Islamic scriptures, and while it is practised in several Islamic countries it is not a custom in most of the Arab world, Pakistan, India or Bangladesh.

The difficulties of understanding a faith are sometimes compounded when insiders to the faith are asked to clarify its teachings, since it can be hard to know when one is getting an individual view or one representing a major division or even a sect. Spokespeople are often men (try to count the religious spokeswomen you have heard of or seen on TV). In addition, with religious groups consisting mainly of immigrants or people of recent immigrant descent, spokes*men* will be those who speak English, and some will be in a position to claim to speak for others by virtue of the internal politics of community groups. They may not genuinely be religious authorities.

ACTIVITY **9.2**

Try to summarise one of the following differences within specific faiths for someone outside it:

- *creationism versus evolution, or Catholic–Protestant hostility;*

- *the differences between Orthodox and Reform Jews;*

- *the distinction between Shi'a and Sunni Islam;*

- *why offerings are made to idols and spirits in supposedly non-theistic Buddhism;*

- *castes within Sikhism;*

- *disputes about untouchability within Hinduism.*

Comment

Depending on their religious background some readers will find at least one of these easy, or at least they will know where to begin. No one would expect a social worker to be familiar with all these internal debates but you might need to look them up one day.

Of necessity I am concerned in this chapter to explain something of the differences between faiths – indeed I have dwelled already on differences within them. It would not be of much practical help simply to say there are lots of similarities, but that's nevertheless the case. All faiths stress moral principles about living a good life and they are not very different: most people want to look after their family, achieve economic security, experience well-being; religions do not conflict with Maslow's hierarchy of needs (Maslow, 1954). Bear that in mind when studying Table 9.2 which aims to summarise key aspects of the world's major faiths. It is based upon wide reading, personal association with people of all the faiths covered, attendance at their religious ceremonies and spending time beyond brief tourism in countries or provinces with Hindu, Muslim, Sikh, Jewish, Buddhist and various kinds of Christian majorities. In case you want to spot any bias, I have no religious belief myself at all. I am not agnostic (uncertain whether there is a god or not), I am an atheist, believing there is none.

ACTIVITY **9.3**

Study Table 9.2 and list four things that you didn't know.

List anything that surprised you.

List anything about which you had a mistaken idea.

Choose one point to explore further from those you have identified above.

Table 9.2 *Summary of key aspects of seven religious groups in Britain*

Faith: UK numbers:	Buddhism 151,000	Christianity 39,500,000	Hinduism 558,000	Islam 1,590,000	Judaism 266,000	Rastafarianism Unknown	Sikhism 335,000
Some key teaching	Five precepts: respect for: life; others' property; our pure nature; honesty; clear mind (no killing, stealing, sexual misconduct, lying, intoxicants)	Treat others as you would wish to be treated, also ten commandments: one God, don't worship idols, don't swear with God's name, rest one special day a week, respect parents, don't lie, murder, commit adultery, or envy others	Too complex and varied to summarise	Five pillars: Allah is the only God and Mohammed was his messenger; pray 5 times daily; fast in daytime 1 month a year; give to the poor; pilgrimage to Mecca once in life	One invisible God the creator, who knows everything and will judge us; belief in the prophets and all the Torah; a Messiah (or Messianic era) will come	God is black, also human, heaven should be on earth, respect planet. Former king of Ethiopia (Haile Selassie) revered as God's incarnation	Devotion to God at all times, truthful living, equality. Avoid: lust, anger, greed, worldly attachment, pride (also superstition and idol worship)
Food, etc.	No absolute restrictions, but some vegetarian	No restrictions	Never beef, many are vegetarian, some vegan	Never pork (some say no seafood except fish); no alcohol, no recreational drugs	Never pork; Orthodox have some strict rules about mixing dairy and meat	Usually vegetarian	Never beef or ritually killed meat; many are vegetarian; no tobacco, no alcohol (latter not strictly observed)
Clothing	No absolute restrictions	Modest dress for females has been traditionally preferred, including covering hair	No absolute restrictions, though female modesty commonplace	Modest dress for females required, legs and hair routinely covered	Modest dress for females traditionally preferred	No absolute restrictions	Modest dress for females traditionally preferred, especially covering legs
Other things worth knowing	Strictly speaking a path or philosophy, since no belief in god	Sunday is holy day	No final leader or authority, a very personal religion observed in thousands of different ways. Inherited status at birth (caste) affects some social mixing, and all marriages	Left hand not used for eating; no images or statues of God; Friday is holy day	No images or statues of God, Saturday is holy day	May use marijuana to aid religious experience. Hair grown in dreadlocks	Five symbols: steel wrist bangle, comb, baggy undershorts, uncut hair (with men's covered by turban), token dagger. Traditional male/female surnames: Singh/Kaur (now used as middle names)

Continued

Table 9.2 continued

Faith: UK numbers:	Buddhism 151,000	Christianity 39,500,000	Hinduism 558,000	Islam 1,590,000	Judaism 266,000	Rastafarianism Unknown	Sikhism 335,000
Membership and conversion	Seldom seek to convert	Central belief of some a duty to convert others. Traditionally, spouses of Catholics expected to convert and children to be raised as Catholic	Seldom seek to convert, except for westernised variants like Hare Krishna and Transcendental Meditation	Central belief of some a duty to convert others and unbelievers are damned. Only supposed to marry Muslims, though Jews or Christians acceptable	No attempt to convert, general belief that born into Judaism, conversion possible but difficult	In practice restricted to black African-Caribbeans and Africans	Rooted in Indian Punjab and Punjabi language, no attempt made to convert and virtually unknown except upon marriage, especially with Hindus
Main subdivisions present in UK	Largely regional, so variations in Indian/ Chinese/ Nepali/Thai Buddhism	Protestant (with dozens of subdivisions) Roman Catholic (third Christian branch, Russian and Greek Orthodox, small in UK)	Huge spectrum of localised beliefs and different images of god. Social divisions (castes) have religious rationale	Sunni (vast majority) Shi'a (mainly Iranian)	Orthodox Reform	None	Fairly unified, but social divisions (castes) have strong cultural power
Historic roots of main groups in UK (in size order)	China Nepal India (Gujarat) Thailand	Protestant: UK, Caribbean, Sub-Saharan Africa Catholic: Ireland, Poland	India (Gujarat and Punjab)	Pakistan (Punjab) Bangladesh (Sylhet) India. Many African countries	Europe (generally over 100 years or more ago)	Caribbean	India (Punjab)
Vernacular languages of main groups in UK	Cantonese Nepali Hindi or Gujarati Thai	English and one or more of dozens of others	Hindi, Gujarati, Punjabi	Urdu, Punjabi Sylheti, Bengali Gujarati. Many African languages, modern Arabic	English	English	Punjabi
Religious language	Pali (understood only by scholars and priests) but vernacular widely used too	English Polish (originally Latin)	Sanskrit (only understood by scholars and priests)	Classical Arabic (not necessarily understood by modern Arabic speakers)	Hebrew, English	Patois or Creole (i.e. Caribbean English)	Old Punjabi (Gurmukhi – not always necessarily understood by worshippers)

Continued

Table 9.2 *continued*

Faith: UK numbers:	Buddhism 151,000	Christianity 39,500,000	Hinduism 558,000	Islam 1,590,000	Judaism 266,000	Rastafarianism Unknown	Sikhism 335,000
Holy book	Tripitaka	New and Old Testament Bible	Vedas, Upanishads, Bhagavad Gita	Koran/ Qur'an	Torah, Talmud, Old Testament Bible	Old Testament Bible	Guru Granth Sahib
Place of worship	Temple; shoes never worn inside	Church or chapel, sometimes houses; men uncover head, in some, women cover theirs	Temple, often altar at home; shoes never worn inside temple	Mosque; shoes never worn inside	Synagogue; women cover hair, men wear Kippah (skull cap)	Homes; hired hall	Gurdwara; shoes never worn inside; men and women cover heads
Title of religious functionary	Priest, perhaps monk. In practice always male	Catholic: priest (addressed as Father) always male Protestant: vicar, minister, sometimes priest, can be female	Priest (in practice always male)	Imam (always male) Mullah (in Shi'ite Islam)	Rabbi	No special title	Granthi (usually male but not always)
Most important festival/s (not the only ones)	Wesak (always May but exact date depends on moon)	Easter (always April but exact date depends on moon); Christmas (25 December in UK tradition but later in others; some regard Christmas Eve as more significant)	Diwali (usually October or November) Holi, spring festival (always late February or March)	Eid-Ul-Fitr, end of fasting month (2010: September) Eid-Ul Adha (2010: November) Both set by lunar year so get earlier each year	Passover (8 days in March/April) Yom Kippur (September/October). (all begin sundown previous day)	Birth of Haile Selassie (23 July)	Vaisakhi 13/14 April) and Guru Nanak's birthday (late October/November) Diwali (October/November) (Some Sikhs use an older lunar calendar with different dates)
How to put your foot in it	Disrespecting Buddha statue – letting your feet point at it, using one as an ornament	Swearing using the name of Jesus	Allowing meat anywhere near a vegetarian Hindu's plate Asking for Christian name	Disrespect to Qur'an or Mohammed Asking for Christian name Serving alcohol	Asking for Christian name	Assuming you can score some weed	Thinking a small boy with a topknot of hair is a girl

Note: Many local authorities and PCTs with significant numbers of people following different faiths publish guides covering customs, rituals, social life, diet, dress, etc. to help practitioners and social care workers. It's worth getting hold of these because they may cover caste/regional/cultural/linguistic variations in religious practices.

Comment

It might be an idea to familiarise yourself with a range of information sources about different faiths so you know where to look when the need arises. It would be more effective to discover things when you need to know them than trying to rote learn strings of facts, but knowing how to avoid putting your foot in it is not too onerous. Websites are excellent sources of details and internal variations within faiths, and can also tell you in advance whether a client's name is, for instance, Muslim, Sikh or Hindu.

CASE STUDY

Bernadette is 67 years old and is progressively more and more affected by Alzheimer's. Her short-term memory is very poor and her three daughters are unable to continue supporting her living in her own house. They all live in the same town but do not have the space within their own homes to take her in. In different ways they have made it clear to you that they barely have space within their own lives, too. The youngest has three school-age children, one has a demanding career, while the other is a lesbian who, while she has great concern for her mother, nevertheless suffered many years of rejection by her mother based upon her religious conviction that being a lesbian was sinful and shameful. She would find it impossible to look after her in her own home which she shares with her partner. The daughters and you have reviewed the care home choices and have a choice of two. One is nearby and would allow easy visiting by Bernadette's daughters. The other is 80 miles away with no convenient motorway link but has the advantage of being run by Irish nuns. In visits to both, Bernadette seemed more at ease in the second, where the accents familiar from her childhood and convent schooling apparently give her comfort. It's unlikely her daughters will be able to visit this second home very often. How would you support the family in making provision for their mother?

Comment

There are numerous Jewish care homes in Britain offering the additional benefit of kosher food aside from other things culturally amenable to older Jews. As yet there are none catering specifically for Muslims, Sikhs or Hindus, partly because it takes decades for any immigrant group to have the same proportion of older people as the original population, but also there is a stronger pattern of joint family living, with different generations sharing housing, income, child and elder care. This is not to repeat the too widely believed cliché that 'they look after their own', too often used to justify poor provision for religious and ethnic minorities. It's worth considering, if all care home provision was secular, what might be lost?

Identity issues

One feature of immigration to Britain in the past 60 years is that, apart from the Irish and (since 2004) the Polish, the vast majority have originated from outside Europe and have not been Christian. The obvious exceptions to this are Caribbean and African Christians, though their style of worship has often been markedly different from British Christianity. A consequence of this has been that whether they liked it or not their identity and sense of themselves was partly imposed upon them: rather than simply being people, they became part of socially distinct groups – black and Asian – marked out as racially different with consequences in terms of worse and lower-paid employment, poor housing opportunities and other forms of discrimination. (This is not the place to justify these assertions, but there is more in the relevant chapter of this book and other suggestions for reading.) Modood (1993) suggests that for decades people were thus defined – and in a sense defined themselves – by their mode of oppression, the basis upon which they received worse treatment, i.e. skin colour. By the 1980s he detected a shift whereby people increasingly chose to define themselves by what was important to them, rather than being defined as Other (by others). Religion played a part in this, he suggests, so rather than accepting labels such as 'Asian' or 'Pakistani' there was a growth in self-recognition and assertion as (for instance) Hindu or Muslim. Events such as 9/11, the Iraq and Afghanistan wars, conflict with Iran and the unresolved Jewish–Muslim conflict in Israel/Palestine makes it increasingly likely that Muslims will position their own identity in relation to these events. (This doesn't mean they routinely support one view or another, but it means it's very hard not to have a view.) It's also the case that non-Muslims with roots in India, who might be mistaken for Muslims on the grounds of physical appearance, may be keen to identify themselves as Hindu or Sikh. (Ironically, the only person killed in the USA in revenge attacks after 9/11 was a Sikh, as were some Asians in Wales whose shop was firebombed (Gaine, 2004).

Value and legal conflicts

I argued above (and in many ways this is borne out by the comparison chart in Table 9.2) that there are many misconceptions about different faiths and that some practices are more to do with culture and tradition than religious law. Nevertheless, there are inescapable conflicts of values in some areas of social life, and social workers may well encounter these. I have summarised below the most common issues where beliefs different from the majority of the population are likely to be underpinned by religion:

- *Abortion* Catholicism; some Protestant groups; Islam to some extent.
- *Contraception* Catholicism; Islam to some extent.
- *Medical care* Christian Scientists and Jehovah's Witnesses oppose blood transfusions.
- *Homosexuality* Catholicism; some Protestant groups; Islam.
- *Polygamy* Islam allows a man up to four wives if they agree and he can support them.
- *Female modesty in dress* Mainly but not exclusively Islam.
- *Male circumcision* Judaism; Islam.
- *Universal laws about self-protection* Sikhs (crash helmets); Rastafarians (marijuana use).
- *Duty to fight in wartime* Quaker Christians.

In each case legislators have wished to pass laws and policy makers to devise policies that cover everyone, but have had to deal with the fact that religious principle will motivate some people to lose their job or go to prison rather than comply. Sikh men, for the most part, want their personal safety to take second place to religious duty by refusing to wear crash helmets on motorbikes (and the law was changed to allow this). Catholic and Muslim medical staff who disapprove of abortion are permitted to opt out of being involved in them. A Muslim woman wearing a full *burqua* is allowed to show her face only to a female passport officer. Whereas a simple refusal to fight landed many men in jail during the Second World War, those doing so for religious reasons were pardoned (many serving as medical orderlies). Male circumcision (unlike removing parts of female genitalia) is required by Islamic and Jewish law, yet except in a minority of cases it serves no medical purpose and must cause infant boys pain. It is allowed under British law and we are very used to the idea, but if it was proposed as a new practice, it would probably be considered abuse.

I do not have a simple formulaic answer for these conflicts of values, and neither will you. The point is that there have always been religious dissenters to supposedly universal laws; such dissent did not arrive with recent immigrants. The simplistic wish that followers of other faiths would be 'just like the British' fails to recognise that the British are not homogenous, and as far as religion is concerned have not been singing from the same hymn sheet for centuries.

Some things are clearer, however, at least in principle. Though the debate was difficult and protracted, it has been decided in recent years that the law giving equal treatment to gay people trumps some aspects of separate religious rights. Catholic adoption agencies are breaking the law if they follow their consciences and discriminate against gay couples seeking to adopt and as a result some have opted to close.

There is also no allowance in British law for abusing people in the name of religion. While there are debates to be had about whether one allows one's daughter to use contraception, one's son to cut his hair or forbids one's entire family to eat meat, abuse by neglect, sexual mistreatment or physical cruelty is unambiguously against the law. Freedom to practise religion does not extend to beating, starving or even killing a child because of a belief it is possessed by devils or is a witch and no social worker should stand back from challenging such practices. I am aware that liberal anxiety, uncertainty and misunderstanding about what some call political correctness can lead to the notion that all standards are culturally relative, but under the standards and the law governing social work they are not.

The controversial and currently topical issue of female dress is something that (literally) gets Islam a lot of bad press. It would be foolish to try to resolve the many arguments surrounding it or to try to have the last word, but there are some things worth considering. While long-established cultural habits are overlaid on people's expectations there is a formal requirement within Islam for women (and men) to dress modestly: loose clothing that doesn't accentuate the body shape is specified, and there is an expectation that women's hair is not casually revealed (Islam shares with Christianity and Judaism a belief from Old Testament times that women are likely to inflame and arouse men, and hair is regarded as playing a big part in this). Muslim scholars and different communities (and social classes) disagree about how much of the face should be covered, with most women's faces visible in Turkey and many in urban Pakistan and Bangladesh (the latter two countries having had unveiled female prime ministers, incidentally, back in the 1980s). For those who perhaps too quickly assume this is all about oppressing women it is worth knowing there is a Muslim feminist argument in favour of Islamic dress, holding that it frees women from the sexual gaze of men and that inside it they experience greater freedom in public than they would if subject to constant male appraisal. Annoyed by the constant portrayal of herself as a victim, a Muslim woman commented of Western women:

> ... whose labour is cheap outside the home and free inside it, whose bodies are commodities and sales incentives in the media, who have no respect if they work and no self respect if they don't, and who are conditioned to go to extraordinary and painful lengths to make their bodies palatable for men – a swift appraisal shows that western women are as oppressed (if more subtly) than their sisters in Islam.

ACTIVITY *9.4*

This is easier if you are female. Get hold of a Muslim woman's full cloak and face covering and wear it for a while in a public place, perhaps as you buy a coffee or something in a shop, or get on a bus. (Do this in your place of study if going out on the street feels too scary.) Reflect on how you are treated compared to your normal everyday experience.

Comment

You may experience two contradictory things: freedom from sexual appraisal simultaneously with palpable Islamophobia. On the latter, depending on where you are in the country and how common such clothing is, you may be largely ignored or get an extreme reaction. It is not easy to get inside the public role of any of the groups covered in this book (though it's possible to spend half a day in a wheelchair, or a straight male could try wearing very obvious makeup). Such experiences can be instructive and make one aware of the invisible knapsack referred to in Chapter 8 on race and ethnicity, but is it ethical? What do members of the group one might pretend to belong to make of it?

Implications

Most of these are covered in the Standards listed at the beginning of this chapter. In some respects recognition of someone's religious beliefs is also the law – for instance in giving employment, in judging whether harassers merit an additional penalty and in awarding a school place. In practice you have no choice: you simply cannot effectively deliver care without taking someone's religious beliefs into account, so it is just not negotiable to ignore them unless they conflict with specific values enshrined in British law. You should take heart from the reassurance that you are not expected to know everything in Table 9.2 in this chapter, let alone the intricacies of many different faiths. What is expected of you, however, is respect for the importance that religion has in people's lives and a positive curiosity about how a person's faith might affect the care you are able to offer them.

C H A P T E R   S U M M A R Y

This chapter has discussed the significance in Britain of established Christianity together with the increase in adherents from other faiths. A good deal of space has been devoted to guidance on what particular faiths believe and do not believe and several comparisons have been drawn between Christianity and currently the most stigmatised of faiths, Islam.

FURTHER READING

Coles, M (2008) *Every Muslim child matters: Practical guidance for schools and children's services*. Stoke-on-Trent: Trentham Books.

The title is a very apt description – a detailed, practical, valuable book.

Crabtree, S A, Husain, F and Spalek, B (2008) *Islam and social work: Debating values, transforming practice*. Bristol: The Policy Press.

A key text and really the only one of its kind, which specifically examines social work with Muslims and the basic tenets of Islam, with specific focus upon the family, education, welfare, gender, health and Islamophobia.

Furness, S and Gilligan, P (2010) *Religion, belief and social work: Making a difference*. Bristol: The Policy Press.

An accessible, comprehensive text which examines the place of religion and belief in everyday social work practice. It provides a valuable resource, practice frameworks and insights to develop culturally sensitive competent practice within a variety of service settings.

Maqsood, R W (1995) *Islam*. Oxford: Heinemann Education.

A clear and illustrated brief guide.

Matthews, I (2009) *Social work and spirituality*. Exeter: Learning Matters.

This text explores the contested historical and contemporary nature of spirituality, the revival of spiritual beliefs and its value and significance for social work practice critically applied within a variety of social work locations.

Moss, B (2005) *Religion and spirituality: Theory into practice*. Lyme Regis: Russell House.

A skilful and sensitively written text which provides an invaluable contribution to our understanding of religion and spirituality. It covers important theoretical ideas and the legislative imperatives and relates them clearly to practice issues while addressing discrimination, oppression, equality and diversity themes.

Ramadan, T (2004) *Western Muslims and the future of Islam*. Oxford: Oxford University Press.

The author is a key intellectual in modern western Islam, immensely well informed and insightful.

WEBSITES

www.bbc.co.uk/religion/tools/calendar/

www.britkid.org

www.insted.co.uk/islam.html

Conclusion

Chris Gaine

This chapter is brief, aiming to draw together some themes from the separate chapters and identify common concerns. The themes are:

- the challenge to common sense;
- how inequality maintains itself at different levels;
- appraisals of institutions and judgements upon individuals;
- personal journeys;
- multiple and combinations of disadvantage.

Common sense and challenging inequality

One theme I want to draw attention to is the disruption of 'common sense' offered by all the chapters. Each chapter challenges everyday assumptions about marginalised groups, and many of these assumptions are founded on simplistic biological ideas, namely:

- Gender is fundamentally determined by sex, so we are programmed into male and female attributes.
- Sexual orientation is biologically decreed as heterosexual; anything else is going against nature, either though madness or badness.
- Age is simply a matter of the body and brain wearing out, becoming less capable and sexless.
- Disability dictates an impaired life; a physical impairment makes one invalid.
- Social class reflects ability, which is largely inborn, so those at the top are just born with more talent (which they probably inherited from their parents who held similar economic positions).
- Race is a biological attribute which really does tell us something of what's beneath the skin, so race and culture are linked – one causes the other.
- Faith is something of the exception here, though there were twentieth-century colonial scientists who argued that non-Europeans were 'naturally' unsuited to the refined and civilised practice of Christianity and of course Nazis believed Jews were biologically predisposed to 'difference' and conversion did nothing to wash out the Semitic stain.

The last of these is the most remote historically, but this should tell us something: there is a tendency to either account for or deny social differences by simplistic appeals to what is 'natural', to biology. These appeals can be very persuasive, but their very appeal should make us wary. The naturalness of common sense is its danger; the seductive ease with which it explains social phenomena is what can make it most oppressive.

Instead, we propose a social model for all the aspects of diversity covered in this book. We argue that the inequality experienced by groups of people is socially, not biologically constructed, that social forces make social distinctions. Thus the book warns us to beware of assumptions that biology puts some of us in the kitchen and others in the garage, that it determines just one pattern of sexual preference, that ageing is just a simple medical fact, that disability is best viewed through a quasi-medical lens, that races are real biological entities. Instead, we argue there is no chronologically determined age when someone passes from not-old to old, there is no exact borderline where one becomes disabled, there is not an absolute boundary between feminine and masculine behaviour, that what matters about skin colour is the social significance it carries. We think the categories have some uses, for example in considering provision, but they should not be prisons because we have built them: they are social constructions. Unsettling though this is, disruptive as it is to common sense, it is an argument with which social workers have to grapple.

Levels of oppression

In doing so, the intricacies of how oppression and inequality work need illuminating. A useful way of looking at this is to think of different levels, especially if considering the presence or absence of prejudice and discrimination in an organisation; these levels are best viewed as personal, cultural, institutional and structural (Gaine, 1989). At the level of the personal, what we are talking about is individual attitudes and their expression; it shades into cultural when individual attitudes and behaviours are understood, tolerated or shared by others. In turn this shades into the institutional level when an organisation operates by the rules and assumptions of a work culture that accepts or even promotes discrimination, and this reaches its most powerful expression at the structural level if institutional prejudice and discrimination is found in the key institutions of the state – politics, the military, the civil service and finally in the laws of the land. Table 10.1 is an illustration of this idea covering two of this book's topics.

Table 10.1 Examples of levels of oppression

	Homophobia	Sexism towards women
Personal	Personal distaste or dislike Avoidance of lesbian and gay people Negative remarks or comments Teasing/bullying/harassment Telling homophobic 'jokes'	Patronising beliefs about women Put downs, negating competence Sexual harassment Telling sexist 'jokes'
Cultural	Shared repertoire of terms of abuse Culture of 'joke' telling and thus Circulation of stereotypes Collective social events exclusion Common stereotypes/assumptions	Shared demeaning terms for women Culture of 'joke' telling and thus Circulation of stereotypes Shared assumptions about childcare, female competence and qualities Resistance to female managers Shared assumptions about dress

Continued

Table 10.1 continued

Institutional	Some awareness of presence of homophobia but no training, few sanctions, not viewed as problematic Denial that culture and climate anything other than 'normal' Homophobia routinely embedded in service functioning and provision	Some awareness of presence of sexism but no training, few sanctions, not viewed as problematic Seniority skewed by gender Denial of problem on any scale Sexism routinely embedded in service functioning and provision
Structural	(until recently) Different partnership laws covering next of kin, inheritance rights, etc. Membership of armed forces Age of consent	Uneven representation in government Legal bar to some occupations

Thompson outlines the same core idea (e.g. 2003, pp13–20) but as concentric circles and without the emphasis on institutional practices and assumptions; he adapted this from Norton (1978).

ACTIVITY 10.1

Make a larger chart and complete the boxes for other aspects of diversity and inequality, or indeed all of them.

Comment

You will find scanning and reviewing previous chapters useful for this and you will find some issues easier to do than others, probably depending on your own personal experience and awareness.

Institutional prejudice and discrimination

Since considerable attention has been given to institutional racism in the past decade following the inquiry into the grossly inadequate police investigation of a black boy's murder (Macpherson, 1999), it's worth considering comparisons with other aspects of inequality since this may also serve to clear up some confusion about institutional processes and responsibility. The chart in Table 10.1 argues that it's possible for an institution to treat groups of people unjustly (unfairly discriminate), not through a planned and deliberate policy or because of the personal prejudice of individuals but because of unexamined assumptions. How can this be? Firstly, I am not denying that it's possible for discrimination to be deliberate; it's possible for the management of a social work department (or school or branch of the police service or the health service) to be aware that key assumptions and attitudes widespread among staff are negative about a specific group and that such attitudes are evident in terminology, common expectations, jokes and procedures. In this case in effect, as a matter of policy, the agency discriminates, unless it works to counter these attitudes and practices.

But it is often not so straightforward. It may be that individual staff express their prejudices (about LGB people for instance) but the institutional culture ignores this, turns a blind eye, accords them the right to their own opinion, doesn't want to make an issue of it, accepts someone as a good colleague despite their words or is intimidated by him/her. This behaviour may be reinforced by occupational culture (or 'canteen culture' as Macpherson called it in the police), 'banter' and loyalty/solidarity with 'one's own', which clearly does not recognise the views, perspectives or feelings of LGB staff (let alone clients). It is not an explicit policy to marginalise, but that is the effect.

Another variant would recognise that prejudice exists in some staff, but they would be assumed to be few, their ideas/practices not endemic or institutionalised and their presence inevitable 'because the service is a cross section of society' (i.e. it does not have specific professional standards). It's the 'bad apples' theory – basically things are okay apart from a few individuals.

Less explicit still, attitudes and assumptions may be expressed in a workplace that unwittingly and unintentionally assume the inferiority, inadequacy, criminality, stupidity, etc. of various groups. This might be prejudice present in individuals and the work culture but which is taken for granted and thus never examined, so in that sense it's unconscious (Travellers can't be trusted, people from that estate are mostly layabouts, Muslim men beat their wives, gay men are promiscuous …).

Finally, institutional discrimination can result from an uncritical and inflexible ethos deriving from 'the established way of doing things' which excludes particular minorities, perhaps through cultural ignorance, lack of appreciation of barriers and disadvantages, unwillingness to believe anything critical of colleagues, compounded lack of trust, a naive idea of 'treating everyone the same'.

Apart from the first (rare and unusual) example, where it is policy to discriminate, the previous four paragraphs show how an organisation can be institutionally discriminating without it being in the hearts and minds of all staff to do so. Therefore to call the Metropolitan Police institutionally racist is not to level a personal accusation at every individual in the service; if a social services department is judged to be ageist it does not mean that its staff knowingly work against the interests of older clients. Typically, assessments of institutional discrimination are about effects, not intentions, and it does not move the debate (or provision) forward an inch for people to protest their individual lack of prejudice.

Personal journeys

Another strand in the book is personal awareness of specific issues and how that inevitably varies. Some readers will have a longer and more difficult journey to make with regard, say, to class prejudices or to providing equitable services to disabled people. As Vini Lander says in Chapter 8 on race and ethnicity:

> If you're White and British, it can be hard to look this topic in the eye and not feel you're being accused of something (and thus get defensive). The opening chapter of this book asserts that everyone has prejudices; this chapter is not implying that in some way Black people are nicer, or more humane, than Whites. You're being asked here to look at things about race and ethnicity you might take for granted, that may be invisible to you, but may be all too visible to someone with a BME background. If comparisons help, female readers might consider how males have a completely

different experience on public transport at night (and may not realise it); someone with good hearing might think how often they have been utterly excluded by a quiet mumbled delivery in a seminar; LGB readers will know about routine assumptions that everyone is heterosexual. These are other forms of invisible knapsacks.

This is not all about familiarity. Different views and approaches to diversity and inequality do not necessarily come about because of greater or lesser familiarity, though they sometimes do. Gender is an aspect of diversity we all know about, we all have experience of, but it does not prevent the stereotyping of men or women. BME people can get tired of someone's protestations of non-racist innocence in terms of 'my best friend is Pakistani …' (as an Indian friend said to me once *that's like saying I can't be sexist because my mother is a woman*). Our general advice would be to evaluate both your own knowledge of a particular group and your own preconceptions about them, to fill in knowledge gaps you have identified from printed materials, from websites and from service users or carers themselves. Perhaps at times someone will marvel at your ignorance, but that's better than marvelling at your arrogance – ignorant people can learn, arrogant people don't think they need to.

This might be a good point to look again at the *Diversity Personal Reflection Plan* suggested as Activity 1.6 in the opening chapter.

Intersectionality

This simply refers to something you will have noticed during the book because the authors have consciously referred to it. People from minority ethnic groups are not completely defined by that fact; being LGB doesn't encapsulate someone's whole identity; it's possible to be old and gay, white and Muslim, disabled and Black, working-class, female and blind, and so on. It seems obvious to say it, but it's vital to remain aware of how different aspects of diversity may intersect within a family or individual. This may entail a celebration of difference, but it may also lead to compounded or multiple disadvantage as one marginalising experience has extra pain added through overt prejudice and is perhaps overlaid with an unresponsive service not recognising unmet needs.

An aspect of intersectionality that can be really troubling is value conflicts that arise for social workers from different aspects of a person's identity. Principles sometimes conflict: how to accept someone vigorously expressing a religious faith that condemns the abortion you may be supporting a client in requesting? How to treat with absolute respect an older person who has neo-Nazi views about people with learning disabilities? What does one say about her derogatory language to an immigrant from a country where gay people are imprisoned? What response can one make to a disabled client who bemoans the money 'wasted' on elder care, or to the mother of a mixed-heritage child who spits out her hostility towards Black men?

Yes, we have left the hardest questions until last.

And finally

While this book dwells a lot on the negative consequences of not recognising diversity, we need to remember a point made in the opening chapter and stated a good deal in Chapter 5 about disability: being different is not inherently a curse; a diverse society is not to be regarded as burdensome or regrettable. It just is – it's the nature of human beings.

Glossary

Attitude Derived from an individual's values, an attitude produces a tendency to react to events in certain ways and to approach or avoid those events that confirm or challenge their values. Attitudes affect individual beliefs and behaviour.

Ageism A network of assumptions, stereotypes and prejudices made on grounds of age, either youth or old age, though in this book we have focused upon older people. Ageism towards older people has a number of dimensions: job discrimination, loss of status, dehumanisation. Ageism can be about assuming that all older people are the same, despite different life histories, needs and expectations. It can affect workers and carers at a personal level; for instance, contact with older people may be avoided as it is viewed as unrewarding or remind younger people of their own ageing. In principle ageism affects young and old, but it can be especially detrimental to older people from the various groups covered in this book since it adds to their already disadvantaged position in society.

Anti-discriminatory practice (ADP) / Anti-oppressive practice (AOP) Important central principles of modern social work practice which stress the need to engage with service users on the basis of how their position may disadvantage, marginalise or oppress them. The dynamics of all the inequalities we deal with in this book and their relationship to mainstream attitudes and behaviours are all relevant to ADP or AOP. Anti-discriminatory practice works with a model of challenging unfairness. Anti-oppressive practice works with a model of empowerment and liberation and requires fundamental rethinking of values, institutions and relationships.

Citizenship A framework of status, rights and obligations within a particular society.

Culture The ideas, values, norms and behaviours associated with a particular social group which shape how we act in and interpret the world. Distinctive cultures can exist in relation to sexual orientation, groups with specific impairments, geographical origins, ethnicity, class, religious groups and more. Culture is never static – it is constantly evolving.

Discrimination Unequal treatment of an individual or group of persons on the basis of features such as race, age, sexual orientation, gender, religion or disability. Discriminating against these groups is unlawful in the UK.

Diversity In principle this simply refers to the range and variety of humanity; however, as discussed in the opening chapter, the diversity that attracts the attention of social policy is that which produces real differences in people's life chances and hence social inequality.

Equal opportunities Though there is no consensus on a precise meaning, it has often described an approach that aims to provide a social environment where people are not excluded from social 'goods' such as education, employment or health care on the basis of unchangeable traits. It's an approach that tends to focus upon equal treatment and respect while tackling discrimination.

Equality Is about making sure people are treated fairly and given fair chances. Equality is not about treating everyone in the same way, but it recognises that their needs are met in different ways. Equality policies focus on those areas covered by the law (see above).

Ethnicity A sense of 'people-hood' based upon one or more of common descent, language, religion and tradition. It has nothing to do with skin colour; white people have ethnicity too.

Ethnocentrism A view of the world where the individual's group is seen as the centre of everything and all other groups are measured (usually negatively) against it.

Gender An individual's personal sense of maleness or femaleness. It is socially constructed (i.e. not 'natural' or just following biological programming) and allocates certain behaviours as fitting male or female roles. This will not always be the same across history, societies, and classes (see also definition of *sex*).

Heteronormativity Strictly speaking means the enforcement of a narrow 'normality' and sameness. However, it tends to be used in a similar way to heterosexism, referring to specifically sexual ideas of normality.

Heterosexism If sexism is the assumption that males are superior to females and rightly exercise more power, than heterosexism is an analogous belief and behaviour about the inherent moral superiority of heterosexuality.

Homophobia Literally 'fear of the same' but it's taken to mean a fear, or phobia, of pretty much anything to do with gay people.

Islamophobia Refers to prejudice and discrimination against Islam or Muslims. Islamophobia has been described as the dread or hatred of Islam and the fear or dislike of all Muslims. It includes the perception that Islam has no values in common with other cultures, is inferior to Western (or Christian) world views and is a violent political ideology rather than a religion.

Labelling Normally the result of stereotyping, labelling involves the attachment of a label (usually a negative attribute) to a group or people.

Marginalise To treat as insignificant or exclude from the mainstream of society.

Meritocracy A system in which success is solely dependent on the merit of an individual.

Misogyny A dislike, or hatred of women.

Multiculturalism A philosophy that acknowledges and values cultural and ethnic diversity in society and thinks there are various tangible (e.g. economic) and intangible (e.g. social) benefits that result from the presence of different types of people who have different beliefs and opinions. It doesn't necessarily argue for the coexistence and acceptance of incompatible values, though it's sometimes portrayed that way.

Patriarchy a system of organising social relations to control and exploit women on personal, institutional, cultural and structural levels.

Positive discrimination Involves discriminating against members of one group to increase the presence of another group known to be unfairly under-represented. Although intended as a way of redressing the balance, it is unlawful in Britain.

Prejudice A learned attitude towards a group of people (and hence individuals from that group) based upon a stereotype and founded more on emotion than rationality and therefore relatively resistant to change. Such attitudes are used to pre-judge people. Strictly speaking it can be positive but it's most commonly meant in the negative sense.

Race A group of people with some biological feature/s that distinguish them from members of other groups, especially when the difference is regarded as socially significant; thus skin colour is widely regarded as demarcating 'races', though eye colour or blood group is not. The biological feature can also be invisible and indeed imaginary, such as the characteristics Nazi racial theorists attributed to Jews. Race is probably a term with more common-sense misunderstandings than any other in this glossary. The key thing to grapple with is that 'races' are socially constructed; however much they seem 'real' they are not categories used by human geneticists.

Racism Racism is the act of discriminating, advantaging or disadvantaging people based on 'race' (often a confused merging of colour, ethnic origin or culture). In order to do this power is needed, and this distinguishes it from racial prejudice.

Religion The world's largest faiths have sets of beliefs focusing on a being that is considered to be supernatural, sacred, divine or of the highest truth. Moral codes, practices, values, institutions, traditions, rituals and scriptures are often traditionally associated with the core belief and give meaning to the believer's experiences of life through reference to an ultimate power or reality.

Sex Refers to matters of biology; a person's sex is usually taken to be a matter of bodily form and hormonal configurations.

Sexism A form of oppression in which men exercise power over women and acquire privileges at their expense. Sexism often characterises social work as 'women's work' linked to caring. Examples of sexist practices or institutional structures would be the condoning of sexual harassment and a workforce where men are more commonly in managerial posts and women in less-well paid and less powerful roles.

Social exclusion Refers not only to poverty and low income but to their causes and consequences. People are said to be social excluded when they experience a combination of linked problems such as unemployment, low educational attainment, low skills, poor housing, bad health and family breakdown. People from the groups covered in this book can also be socially excluded when they face barriers that other people do not face that prevent their access to services and their participation in community life.

Stereotyping The process that leads to generalisations concerning the characteristics of a particular group of people. It's usually resistant to any contrary evidence and is a key component of prejudice.

Transgender The physical characteristics of one sex with the psychological characteristics of another.

References

Abbott, P and Meerabeau, L (eds) (1998) *The sociology of the caring professions.* London: University College London Press.

Acker, S and Feuerverger, G (1996) Doing good and feeling bad: The work of women university teachers. *Cambridge Journal of Education*, 26 (3), 401–22.

Adams, M, Bell, L A, Griffin, P (ed) (2007) *Teaching for diversity and social justice. 2nd edition. New York and Abingdon: Routledge/Taylor & Francis Group.*

Ahmed, T (1998) The Asian experience. In Rawaf, S and Bahl, V (eds) *Assessing health needs of people from minority ethnic groups.* London: Royal College of Physicians.

Alcock, P (2003) *Social policy in Britain.* 2nd edition. Basingstoke: Palgrave.

Arnot, M (1986) Cited in Beechey, V and Whitelegg, E (eds) *Women in Britain today.* Buckingham: Open University Press.

Atkinson, D and Williams, F (eds) (1990) *Know me as I am: An anthology of prose, poetry and art by people with learning difficulties.* London: Hodder & Stoughton.

Audit Commission (2004) *The journey to race equality.* London: Audit Commission.

Bagilhole, B (2009) *Understanding equal opportunities and diversity: The social differentiations and intersections of equality.* Bristol: The Policy Press.

Bagilhole, B and Cross, C (2006) 'It never struck me as female': Investigating men's entry into female-dominated occupations. *Journal of Gender Studies*, 15 (1), 35–48.

Banks, S (2006) Ethics and values in social work. 3rd edition. Basingstoke: Palgrave Macmillan.

Barker, R (1997) *Political Ideas in modern Britain: In and after the 20th Century.* London: Routledge.

Beiver, C (2009) The making of a savant. *New Scientist*, 6 June, pp30–1.

Benson, J (2003) *Working class in Britain, 1850–1939.* London: I B Tauris.

Beresford, P and Trevillion, S (1995) *Developing skills for community care: A collaborative approach.* London: Arena.

Beveridge, W (Chair) (1942) *Report of the inter-departmental committee on social insurance and allied services.* Cmnd 6404. The Beveridge Report. London: HMSO.

Birkhead, T (2001) *Promiscuity: An evolutionary history of desire.* Cambridge, MA: Harvard University Press.

Blastland, M (2008) **news.bbc.co.uk**.

Brandon, T and Elliott, A (2008) The art of affirming identity. In Swain, J and French, S (eds) *Disability on equal terms*. London: Sage, pp90–103.

Bromley, D and Longino, C F (1972) *White racism and black Americans*. Cambridge, MA: Schenkman.

Brooks, N, et al. (2000) Asian patients' perspective on the communication facilities provided in a large inner city hospital. *Journal of Clinical Nursing*, 9 (5), 706–12.

Brown Cosis, H (1998) *Social work and sexuality*. Basingstoke: Macmillan.

Browne, N (2004) *Gender equity in the early years*. Maidenhead: Open University Press.

Butler, J (1993) Bodies that matter. On the discursive limits of sex. Cited in Ward, R, Vass, A A, Garfield, C and Cybyk, B (2005) A kiss is still a kiss? *Dementia*, 4 (1), 49–72.

Butler, J (1998) Merely cultural. *New Left Review*, 227, 33–45.

Butt, J (2006) Are we there yet? *Identifying the characteristics of social care organisations that successfully promote diversity*. London: SCIE.

Butt, J and Dhaliwal, S (2005) *Different paths: Challenging services*. London: Habinteg Housing Association, ASRA Greater London Housing Association and the Housing Corporation.

Cabinet Office Social Exclusion Task Force (2008) *Aspiration and attainment amongst young people in deprived communities: Analysis and discussion paper.* London: Social Exclusion Task Force.

Cambridgeshire Parliament of People with Learning Disabilities (2008) *A life like any other? Human rights of adults with learning disabilities. Seventh Report of Session.* Statement to Joint Committee on Human Rights para. 222. London: The Stationery Office.

Cannadine, D (2000) *Class in Britain*. London: Penguin.

Care of Children Committee (1946) *The Curtis Report.* Cmd 6922. London: HMSO.

Carr, S and Dittrich, R (2008) *Personalisation: A rough guide* (Report 20). London: SCIE.

Carr, S and Robbins, D (2009) The implementation of individual budget schemes in adult social care. SCIE, at: **www.scie.org.uk/publications**.

Cemlyn, S, Greenfields, M, Burnett, S, Matthews, Z and Whitwell, C (2009) *Inequalities experienced by gypsy and traveller communities: A review*. Manchester: Equality and Human Rights Commission.

Chahal, K and Ullah, A L (2004) *Experiencing ethnicity: Discrimination and service provision*. York: Joseph Rowntree Foundation.

Charlesworth, S (2000) *Phenomenology of working class experience*. Port Chester, NY: Cambridge University Press.

Christie, A (2001) Gendered discourses of welfare, men and social work. In Christie, A (ed.) *Men in social work*. Basingstoke: Palgrave.

Clark, L (2002) *Accessible health information: Project report*. Liverpool: Central Liverpool NHS Primary Care Trust.

Clarke, G (1998) Voices from the margins: regulation and resistance in the lives of lesbian teachers. In Erben, M (ed.) *Biography and education: A reader.* Lewes: Falmer Press.

Clarke, J and Newman, J (1997) *The managerial state.* London: Sage.

Clements P and Spinks T (2008) *The equal opportunities handbook: How to deal with everyday issues of unfairness.* 4th edition. London: Kogan Page.

Coffey, A and Delamont, S (2000) *Feminism and the classroom teacher*. London: Routledge Falmer.

Coles, M (2008) *Every Muslim child matters: Practical guidance for schools and children's services.* Stoke-on-Trent: Trentham Books.

Commission for Social Care Inspection (2008) *Putting people first: Equality and diversity matters.* London: Commission for Social Care Inspection.

Commission for Social Care Inspection (2009) *Putting people first: Equality and diversity matters 3 – Achieving disability equality in social care services.* London: CSCI.

Committee of the Secondary Schools Examination Council (1943) *Curriculum and examinations in secondary schools*. The Norwood Report. London: HM Stationery Office.

Committee on Homosexual Offences and Prostitution (1957) *Report of the committee on homosexual offences and prostitution.* Cmnd 247. The Wolfenden Report. London: HMSO.

Concannon, L (2009) Developing inclusive health and social care policies for older LGBT citizens. *British Journal of Social Work*, 39, 403–17.

Connell, R W (2006) Understanding men: Gender sociology and the new international research on masculinities. In Skelton, C, Francis, B and Smulyan, L (eds) *The Sage handbook of gender and education.* London: Sage.

Corker, M (1996) *Deaf transitions: Images and origins of deaf families, deaf communities and deaf identities*. London: Jessica Kingsley.

Corker, M and Shakespeare, T (2002) *Disability/postmodernity: Embodying disability theory*. London: Continuum.

Crabtree, S A, Husain, F and Spalek, B (2008) *Islam and social work: Debating values, transforming practice.* Bristol: The Policy Press.

Cranmer, T and McCray, J (2009) Skills for collaborative working. In Mantell, A. (ed.) *Social work skills with adults*. Exeter: Learning Matters.

Cummings, E and Henry, W (1961) *Growing old: The process of disengagement.* New York: Basic Books.

Dalrymple, J and Burke, B (2006) *Anti-oppressive practice: Social care and the law.* Maidenhead: Open University Press.

Darke, P (1998) Understanding cinematic representations of disability. In Shakespeare, T (ed.) *The disability reader: Social science perspectives.* London: Cassell, pp181–97.

Davies, B (1989) *Frogs and snails and feminist tales.* Sydney: Allen & Unwin.

Davies, K (1993) The crafting of good clients. In Swain, J, Finkelstein, V, French, S and Oliver, M (eds) *Disabling barriers: Enabling environments.* 1st edition. London: Open University Press/Sage, pp197–200.

Denzin, N K (1989) *Interpretive biography.* Newbury Park, CA: Sage.

Department for Communities and Local Government (2007) *Guidance on new measures to outlaw discrimination on grounds of sexual orientation in the provision of goods, facilities and services.* London: Department for Communities and Local Government.

Department for Education and Skills (2005) *Ensuring the attainment of white working-class boys in writing.* DfES, at: **www.nationalstrategies.standards.dcsf.gov.uk**.

Department of Education and Science (1967) *Children and their primary schools.* The Plowden Report. London: HMSO.

Department of Education and Science (1995) *Sex Discrimination Act.* London: HMSO.

Department of Health (1995) *Disability Discrimination Act.* London: HMSO.

Department of Health (2000a) *Carers (Recognition and Services) Act.* London: The Stationery Office.

Department of Health (2000b) *National service framework for older people.* London: The Stationery Office.

Department of Health (2001a) *Nothing about us without us.* London: Department of Health.

Department of Health (2001b) *Valuing people: A new strategy for learning disability for the 21st century.* London. HMSO.

Department of Health (2005) *Valuing people: The story so far.* London: HMSO.

Department of Health (2007) *Report of the learning disability task force.* London: Department of Health.

Department of Health (2008a) *Transforming social care.* LAC (1). London: Department of Health.

Department of Health (2008b) *Putting people first.* London: The Stationery Office.

Department of Health (2009) *Valuing people now: The delivery plan.* London: Department of Health.

Dick, S (2008) *Homophobic hate crime: The British gay crime survey.* London: Stonewall.

Dominelli, L (2002) *Anti-oppressive social work theory and practice*. London: Macmillan.

Du Gay, P (ed.) (1997) *Production of culture/cultures of production. London:* Open University with Sage.

Dunant, S (ed.) (1994) *The war of the words: The political correctness debate*. London: Virago.

Dyhouse, C (1981) *Girls growing up in late Victorian and Edwardian England*. London: Routledge.

Ellison, G and Gunstone, B (2009) *Sexual orientation explored: A study of identity, attraction, behaviour and attitudes in 2009.* Manchester: Equality and Human Rights Commission.

Employment Equality (Age) Regulations 2006 in England, Wales and Scotland. London: The Stationery Office.

Epstein, D, Elwood, J, Hey, V and May, J (1998) *Failing boys? Issues in gender and achievement.* Buckingham: Open University Press.

Equality Act 2006. London: The Stationery Office.

Equality and Human Rights Commission (2009) *Beyond tolerance: Making sexual orientation a public matter.* London: EHRC.

Erben, M (1998) Biography and research method. In Erben, M (ed.) *Biography and education: A reader.* Lewes: Falmer Press.

Erikson, E (1977) *Childhood and society.* London: Paladin.

Evans, R and Banton, M (2001) *Learning from experience: Involving black people in shaping services.* Coventry: Council of Disabled People.

Flynn, R (2002) *Short breaks: Providing better access and more choice for black disabled children and their parents.* Bristol: The Policy Press for the Joseph Rowntree Foundation. (See also Flynn, R (2002) Providing better access to short breaks for black disabled children and their parents. *JRF Findings*, 582, online at: **www.jrf.org.uk**.)

Francis, B (1999) Modernist reductionism or post-structural relativism: Can we move on? An evaluation of the arguments in relation to feminist educational research. *Gender and Education*, 11, 4.

Francis, B (2006) The nature of gender. In Skelton, C, Francis, B and Smulyan, L (eds) *The Sage handbook of gender and education.* Sage: Routledge

Francis, B and Skelton, C (2005) *Reassessing gender and achievement: Questioning contemporary key debates.* Abingdon: Routledge.

Fraser, N (1998) Comment: Heterosexism, misrecognition and capitalism, a response to Judith Butler. *New Left Review*, 228, 140–9.

Friedson, E (1994) *Professionalism reborn: Theory, prophecy and policy*. Cambridge: Polity Press.

Frost, R (1936) Provide, provide. In Ferguson, M, Salter, M and Stallworthy, J (eds) (2005) *The Norton anthology of poetry*. 5th edition. New York: W W Norton.

Furness, S and Gilligan, P (2010) *Religion, belief and social work: Making a difference*. Bristol: The Policy Press.

Gaine, C (1989) On getting equal opportunities and keeping them. In Cole, M (ed.) *Education for equality*. London: Routledge.

Gaine, C (2004) *Minority ethnic experience in Herefordshire*. Chichester: University of Chichester.

Gaine, C (2005) *We're all white thanks*. Stoke-on-Trent: Trentham Books.

Gender Equality Duty (2007) London: HMSO.

George, A (2009) Welcome to the universe kids. *New Scientist*, March, pp24–5.

Gerhardt, S (2004) *Why love matters: How affection shapes a baby's brain*. London: Routledge.

Mir, G, Nocon, A, Ahmad, W and Jones, L (2001) *Learning difficulties and ethnicity*. London: Department of Health.

Gillborn, D (1990) *Race ethnicity and education: Teaching and learning in multiethnic schools*. London: RoutledgeFalmer.

Gillborn, D and Mirza, H (2000) *Educational inequality: Mapping race, class and gender*. London: OfSTED.

Gillman, M, Swain, J and Heyman, B (1997) Life history or 'case' history: the objectification of people with learning difficulties through the tyranny of professional discourses. *Disability and Society*, 12 November.

Glasby, J (2009) Commentary on personalisation. *Community Care*, 28 May, p28.

Goble, C (2000) Partnership in residential settings. In Astor, R and Jeffries, K (eds) *Positive initiatives for people with learning difficulties: Promoting healthy lifestyles*. Basingstoke: Macmillan.

Golightley, M (2008) *Social work and mental health*. 3rd edition. Exeter: Learning Matters.

Government Equalities Office (2009) *A fairer future: The Equality Bill and other action to make equality a reality*. London: GEO Publications.

Graham, M (2007) *Black issues in social work and social care*. Bristol: The Policy Press.

Gray, B and Ridden, G (1999) *Lifemaps of people with learning disabilities*. London: Jessica Kingsley.

Gross, R (1995) *Psychology: The science of mind and behaviour*. London: Hodder & Stoughton.

Grover, B (1997) Growing up white in America? In Delgado, R and Stefancic, J (eds) *Critical white studies looking behind the mirror*. Philadelphia, PA: Temple University Press.

GSCC (2004) *Code of practice for social care workers and Code of practice for employ-ers of social care workers.* London: GSCC.

Guasp, A (2009) *The teachers' report. Homophobic bullying in Britain's schools.* London: Stonewall.

Hall, B (2009) Managing the self. In Mantell, A (ed.) *Social work skills with adults.* Exeter: Learning Matters.

Hart, C, Shane, C, Spencer, K and Still, A (2007) *Our lives, our communities: Promoting independence and inclusion for people with learning difficulties.* York: Joseph Rowntree Foundation.

Hill, H and Kenyon, R (2008) *Promoting equality and diversity.* Oxford: Oxford University Press.

Hills, J (2004) *Inequality and the state.* Oxford: Oxford University Press.

Hiro, D (1992) *Black British, white British.* London: Paladin.

Home Office (2005) *Race equality in public services.* London: Race, Cohesion, Equality and Faith Directorate.

hooks, b (2000) *Where we stand: Class matters.* London: Routledge.

Hughes, J (2009) *Are separate schools divisive? A case study from Northern Ireland.* Paper presented at the European Conference on Educational Research, Vienna, September.

Hunt, R and Cowan, K (2009) *Monitoring sexual orientation in the health sector.* London: Department of Health.

Hunt, R and Dick, S (2008) *Serves you right: Lesbian and gay people's expectations of discrimination.* London: Stonewall.

Hunt, R and Jensen, J (2007) *The school report. The experiences of young gay people in Britain's schools.* London: Stonewall.

Hunt, R, Cowan, K and Chamberlain, B (2007) *Being the gay one: Experiences of lesbian, gay and bisexual people working in the health and social care sector.* London: Stonewall.

International Federation of Social Workers (2004) General meeting proposal for a new ethical document. Agenda Item 11.1. Online at: **www.ifs.org/GM-2004/GM-Ethics.html**.

Joint Committee on Human Rights (2008) *A life like any other? Human rights of adults with learning disabilities. Seventh Report of Session.* London: The Stationery Office.

Jones, C (1999) *Poverty, welfare and the disciplinary state.* London: Routledge.

Jones, R (1999) *Teaching racism or tackling it? Multicultural stories from beginning white teachers.* Stoke-on-Trent: Trentham Books.

Kamm, J (1965) *Hope deferred: Girls' education in English history.* London: Methuen.

Kessler, S and McKenna, W (1978) *Gender: An ethnomedographical approach.* Chicago, IL: University of Chicago Press.

King, J E (2004) Dyconscious racism: ideology, identity and the miseducation of teachers. In Ladson-Billings, G and Gillborn, D (eds) *The RoutledgeFalmer reader in multicultural education.* Abingdon: RoutledgeFalmer.

King, M and Bartlett, A (1999) British psychiatry and homosexuality. *British Journal of Psychiatry,* 175, 106–13.

Knott, C and Scragg, T (2007) *Reflective practice in social work.* Exeter: Learning Matters.

Knowles, G (2009) *Ensuring every child matters.* London: Sage.

Lawrence, S and Simpson, G (2009) International aspects of social work with elders. In Lawrence, S, Lyons, K, Simpson, G and Huegler, N (eds) *Introducing international social work.* Exeter: Learning Matters.

Leonard, P (1997) *Postmodern welfare: Reconstructing an emancipatory project.* London: Sage.

Lewis, J (1984) *Women in England 1870–1950: Sexual divisions and social change.* Hemel Hempstead: Wheatsheaf Books.

McAll, C (1992) *Class, ethnicity and social inequality.* Montreal: McGill-Queen's University Press.

McGee, J and Menolacino, F (1991) *Beyond gentle teaching: A non-aversive approach to helping those in need.* London: Plenum Press.

McIntosh, P (1990) White privilege: unpacking the invisible knapsack. *Independent School,* Winter, 31–6.

MacNaughton, G (2000) *Rethinking gender in early childhood education.* London: Paul Chapman Publishing.

Macpherson, W (1999) *The Stephen Lawrence inquiry: Report of an inquiry by Sir William Macpherson of Cluny.* Cm 4262-I. London: The Stationery Office.

Madoc-Jones, B and Coates, J (eds) (1996) *An introduction to women's studies.* Oxford: Blackwell.

Mantell, A (ed.) (2009) *Social work skills with adults.* Exeter: Learning Matters.

Manthorpe, J S, Jacobs, J, Rapaport, D J, Challis, A P, Netten, C, Glendinning, M, Stevens, M, Wilberforce, M and Harris, J (2009) *Evaluation of individual budgets pilots.* London: Department of Health.

Maqsood, R W (1995) *Islam.* Oxford: Heinemann Education.

Marx, S (2006) *Revealing the invisible confronting passive racism in teacher education.* New York: Routledge Taylor & Francis Group.

Maslow, A (1954) *Motivation and personality.* New York: Harper & Row.

Matthews, I (2009) *Social work and spirituality*. Exeter: Learning Matters.

Mirza, H (ed.) (1997) *Black British feminism*. London: Routledge.

Modood, T (1993) *Not easy being British.* London: Runnymede Trust.

Moss, B (2005) *Religion and spirituality: Theory into practice.* Lyme Regis: Russell House.

Mumtaz, K and Shaheed, F (1987) *Women of Pakistan.* London: Zed Books.

Namaganda, S (2004) *Information for people with learning disabilities from Black and minority ethnic groups.* York: Norah Fry Research Centre.

Nash, P (2008) *We are all middle class now.* Online at: **www.teachersupport.info/news**.

Neath, J and Schriner, K (1998) Power to people with disabilities: Empowerment issues in employment. *Disability and Society*, 13(3), 217–28.

Neely-Barnes, S L , Marcenko, M O and Weber, L A (2008) Community-based, consumer directed services: Differential experiences of people with mild and severe intellectual disabilities. *Social Work Research*, 32(1), 55–64.

Norton, D G (1978) *The dual perspective: Inclusion of ethnic minority content in the social work curriculum*. Washington, DC: Council for Social Work Education.

O'Donnell, M and Sharpe, S (2000) *Uncertain masculinities*. London and New York: Routledge.

Office for National Statistics (2004) *Focus on ethnicity and identity*. London: ONS.

Office for National Statistics (2006) Online at: **www.statistics.gov.uk/**.

Office for National Statistics (2007) Online at: **www.statistics.gov.uk/cci/nugget.asp?id=322**.

Office for National Statistics (2009) Standard Occupational Classification 2000. Online at: **www.ons.gov.uk/about-statistics**.

Oko, J (2008) *Understanding and using theory in social work.* Exeter: Learning Matters.

Oliver, M (1993) Disability: A creation of industrialised societies? In Swain, J, Finkelstein, V, French, S and Oliver, M (eds) *Disabling barriers: Enabling environments.* 1st edition. London: Sage, in association with the Open University.

Oliver, M (1996) *Understanding disability: From theory to practice*. Basingstoke. Macmillan.

Ossowski, S (1998) *Class structure in the social consciousness.* London: Routledge.

Owen, M and Farmer, E (1995) *Child protection practice: private risks and public remedies: A study of decision-making, intervention and outcome in child protection work*. London: HMSO.

Paechter, C (2001) Using poststructuralist ideas in gender theory and research. In Francis, B and Skelton, C (eds) *Investigating gender: Contemporary perspectives in education*. Buckingham: Open University Press.

Parekh, B (2000) *The future of multiethnic Britain. The Parekh Report*. London: Runnymede Trust.

Parton, N and O'Byrne, P (2000) *Constructive social work: Towards a new practice?* Basingstoke: Macmillan and St. Martin's Press.

Payne, M (1995) *Social work and community care*. Basingstoke: Palgrave Macmillan.

Pearce, S (2005) *You wouldn't understand: White teachers in multiethnic classrooms*. Stoke-on-Trent: Trentham Books.

Pennington, D C (2000) *Social cognition*. London: Routledge.

Perry, R W and Cree, V E (2003) The changing gender profile of applicants to qualifying social work training in the UK. *Social Work Education*, 22(4), 377–83.

Poverty Site (2009) Online at: **www.poverty.org.uk/summary/**.

Preston, G (2008) *2 skint 4 school*. London: Child Poverty Action Group.

Pugh, S (2008) Back in the closet – the care system and older lesbians, gay men and bisexuals. In *Equality law and older people*. London: Stonewall.

Purvis, J (1995) *Women's history of Britain, 1850–1945*. London: UCL Press.

Quereshi, T, Berridge, D and Wenmen, H (2000) *Where to turn? Family support for South Asian Communities*. London: National Children's Bureau.

Race Relations (Amendment) Act 2000. Available at: **www.opsi.gov.uk/acts**.

Ramadan, T (2004) *Western Muslims and the future of Islam*. Oxford: Oxford University Press.

Ramcharan, P (ed.) (1997) *Empowerment in everyday life: Learning difficulties*. London: Jessica Kingsley.

Refugee and Migrant Justice (2009) *Does every child matter? Children seeking asylum in Britain*. London: Refugee and Migrant Justice.

Rice, B and Savage, T (2006) *Against the odds*. London: Shelter.

Riddell, M (1998) Statisticians tell us that we're all middle class now – but that doesn't stop poorer people dying younger. Online at: **www.newstatesman.com/**.

Runnymede Trust (1997) *Islamophobia: A challenge for us all*. London: Runnymede Trust.

Ryde, J (2009) *Being white in the helping professions: Developing effective intercultural awareness*. London: Jessica Kingsley.

Sampson, E (1993) *Celebrating the other: A dialogic account of human nature*. Hemel Hempstead: Harvester Wheatsheaf.

Schweitzer, P and Bruce, E (2008) *Remembering yesterday, caring today*. London: Jessica Kingsley.

Seebohm, F (Chair) (1968) *Report of the committee on local authority and allied personal social services*. The Seebohm Report. London: HMSO.

Sexual Offences Act 1967. London: The Stationery Office.

Sexual Offences Act 2000. London: The Stationery Office.

Sharpe, S (1976) *Just like a girl*. London: Penguin.

Sheppard, M, Newstead, S, DiCaccavo, A and Ryan, K (2001) Comparative hypothesis assessment and quasi triangulation as process knowledge assessment strategies in social work practice. *British Journal of Social Work*, 31(6), 863–85.

Singh, B (2005) *Making change happen for black and minority ethnic disabled people*. York: Joseph Rowntree Foundation.

Skeggs, B (2002) *Formations of class and gender: Becoming respectable*. London: Sage.

Skelton, C and Francis, B (eds) (2003) *Boys and girls in the primary classroom*. Buckingham: Open University Press.

Skelton, C and Francis, B (2009) *Feminism and 'the schooling scandal'*. Abingdon: Routledge.

Smethurst, C (2007) Gender and reflective practice. In Knott, C and Scragg, T (eds) *Reflective practice in social work*. 2nd edition. Exeter: Learning Matters.

Smith, A and Calvert, J (2001) *Opening doors: Working with older lesbians and gay men*. London: Age Concern.

Stacey, M (1992) *Regulating British medicine: The General Medical Council.* Chichester: John Wiley & Sons.

Stanworth, M (1981) *Gender and schooling*. London: Hutchinson.

Stobbs, P (2008) *Extending inclusion: Council for disabled children*. London: DCSF.

Stonewall (2009) *What's it got to do with you?* London: Stonewall.

Stuart, O (2006) *Will community-based support services make direct payments a viable option for black and minority ethnic service users and carers?* Race Equality discussion paper 1. London: Social Care Institute for Excellence.

Swain, J and French, S (2008) *Disability on equal terms.* London: Sage.

Swain, J, French, S and Cameron, C (2003) *Controversial issues in a disabling society*. Buckingham: Open University Press.

Tajfel, H and Turner, J (1979) An integrative theory of intergroup conflict. In Austin, W G and Worchel, S (eds) *The social psychology of intergroup relations*. Monterey, CA: Brooks-Cole, pp94–109.

Tanner, D and Harris, J (2008) *Working with older people.* Abingdon: Routledge.

Thompson, B (2006) Gender issues in the primary classroom. In Knowles, G (ed.) *Supporting inclusive practice.* London: David Fulton.

Thompson, J (2000) *Women, class and education.* London: Routledge.

Thompson, N (2001) *Promoting equality: Challenging discrimination and oppression.* Basingstoke: Palgrave Macmillan.

Thompson, N (2003) *Promoting equality: Challenging discrimination and oppression.* 2nd edition. Basingstoke: Palgrave Macmillan.

Thompson, N (2006) *Anti-discriminatory practice.* 4th edition. Basingstoke: Palgrave.

Thompson, N (2009) *Promoting equality, valuing diversity – A learning and development manual.* Lyme Regis: Russell House.

Thomson, K (ed.) (2003) *British social attitudes – The 20th report: Continuity and change over two decades.* London: Sage.

Topss UK Partnership (2002) *National occupational standards for social work.* Leeds: General Social Care Council.

Trivedi, B (2009) Autistic and proud. *New Scientist*, June, pp36–40.

Turnball, A (2002) *Opening doors: The needs of older lesbians and gay men.* London: Age Concern.

Walker, A and Northmore, S (2005) *Growing older in a black and ethnic minority group.* London: Age Concern.

Walmsley, J (2002) Principles and types of advocacy. In Gray, B and Jackson, R (eds) *Advocacy and learning disability.* London: Jessica Kingsley.

Ward, L and Carvel, J (2008) Goodbye married couples, hello alternative family arrangements. *Guardian*, 23 January.

Ward, R, Vass, A A, Garfield, C and Cybyk, B (2005) A kiss is still a kiss? *Dementia*, 4 (1), 49–72.

Warwick, I, Chase, E, Aggleton, P and Sanders, S (2004) *Homophobia, sexual orientation and schools: A review and implications for action.* Research Report RR594. London: DCFS.

Wheen, F (2000) *Karl Marx.* London: Fourth Estate.

Wilkinson, R and Pickett, K (2010) *The spirit level: why equality is better for everyone.* London: Penguin.

Wright, E O (2000) *Class counts.* Port Chester, NY: Cambridge University Press.

Websites

www.bbc.co.uk/religion/tools/calendar

www.britkid.org

www.insted.co.uk/islam.html

www.multiverse.ac.uk

www.multiverse.ac.uk/attachments/TalkingRaceSite/index.html

www.pfc.org.uk/files/monitoring_sexual_orientation_in_the_health_sector.pdf

www.scottishmediamonitor.com/articles.cfm

www.statistics.gov.uk/downloads/theme_population/Table_1_Summary_of_
marriages.xls

Index

activity theory 48
age discrimination 43–4
ageing theories 46–50
ageism 44–6
  and common sense 116
AIDS 31–2
Anglicanism 103, 104
asylum seekers 100–1
Atkinson, Dorothy 59
Autistic Spectrum Disorder 59–60

Black and minority ethnic (BME) 92

caring script 20
categorisation 4
Christianity 103, 104, 106
circumcision 113
'coloured' as racial term 91
Commission for Racial Equality 93
common sense 116–17
continuity theory 48
control/power strategies 5*Fig*
cultural racism 92
Curtis Report 21

difference *see* diversity
disability 56–64
  affirmative model 56, 58–9
    case studies 59–60
    evidence review 60–1
    practice implications 61–2
  collaborative culture 63–4
  and common sense 116
  dialogue-based approach 62
  and impairment 57
  personal tragedy model 57–8, 59
  social model 56–7

  origins/development 57–8
  strengths/abilities approach 62–3
  see also learning disabilities
Disability Discrimination Act (1995) 56
discrimination 4
disengagement theory 47–8
diversity
  key concepts 3–4
  personal awareness 119–20
  perspective changes 6–7
  relevance of differences 4–6
  social model 117
  value 2, 121
dysconscious racism 96

elegant challenging 11
The Empire Windrush 89
Equal Pay Act (1970) 31
equality *see* inequality
Equality and Human Rights Commission 14
Erikson's life cycle 47
ethnicity
  ethnic group 92
  see also race
evangelicals 104

faith *see* religion
feelings and attitudes 2
females
  genital mutilation 106, 113
  see also gender
fundamentalism 104, 106

gender
  assumptions about social workers 22–3
  basic issues 18–19
  and common sense 116

difference and social policy 20–1
historical framework 20–1
identity 19–20
innate difference 25–6
law 27–8
relational theory 26–7
role 20
socially constructed roles 26
stereotype persistence 24–5
terminology 19
theories 25–7
see also sexual orientation
genital mutilation 106, 113
Grandin, Prof Temple 59–60
group practice competence 50
Gypsy Roma and Traveller Groups 94, 95–6

hate crime 37
Hawking, Stephen 58
hierarchy of needs 107
HIV/AIDS 31–2
homophobia 31–2, 33, 37–40
implications for social workers 39–40
workplace 37–8
honour killings 106
Human Rights Act (1998) 56

identification 4
identity management theory 48
impairment 57
inequality
and common sense 116–17
different laws 13–14
dimensions 11–13
harmonisation of law 14
law revision 11
personal awareness 119–20
institutional prejudice 118–119
institutional racism 92–3, 118, 119
intersectionality 120
Islam
and female dress 113–14
identity 112
images of 105–6
Islamic/Islamist 104
Islamophobia 92

Lawrence, Stephen 92
learning disabilities 67–74
background 67
culturally specific practice 70–3

influencing change 73–4
personalised care defined 68–9
valued practice defined 67–8
see also disability
lesbian, gay and bisexual (LGB) 31, 120
attitudes to 39–40, 118
levels of oppression 117–18
life course theory 48

Macpherson Report 92–3, 118
male circumcision 113
Marx, Karl 11–12, 76–7
Maslow's hierarchy of needs 107
Mental Capacity Act (2007) 56
minority ethnic 92
Muslim issues *see* Islam

nature/nurture debate 25–6
new age beliefs 103
Northern Ireland 103
Norwood Report 21

Office for National Statistics (ONS) 78
older people 43–53
age discrimination 43–4
ageism 44–6
basic issues 43–6
definition of old age 43
legislation and policy 51 *Table*
social policy and 50–3
theories of ageing 46–50
oppression, levels of 117–18

paedophilia 36
Patmore, Coventry 20
person-centred practice 50
Plowden Report 21
political correctness 8–11, 98–9
poverty 85–6
prejudice 3–4
institutional 118–119
professional development x
Protestants 104
psychological distinctiveness 4

race 89–98
background 89
and common sense 116
deficit model 97
and law 93–4

multicultural Britain 89–90
  social workers and 96–8
  terminology 91–3
Race Relations Acts 93
racism 92, 96
reflective practice x
religion 103–14
  abusing people in the name of 113
  and common sense 116–17
  definitions/terminology 104
  faith survey 103
  identity issues 111–12
  key faith aspects 108–10 *Table*
  preconceptions/misconceptions 104–7
  and social workers 114
  value/legal conflicts 112–14
Roman Catholics 104
Ruskin, John 20

sects 104
secular society 103, 104
Sex Discrimination Act (1975) 21, 27
sex role theory 26
sexual orientation 30–40
  causes of difference 36
  changing attitudes 30–4
  and common sense 116
  dual identities 32
  monitoring of numbers 34–5
  and paedophilia 36
  timeline 33–4 *Table*
  see also gender

social class 76–86
  basic definition 76
  categories (SOC) 78–9
  and common sense 116
  cultural factors 80–3
  economic factors 76–80
  and inequality 12
  and poverty 85–6
social identity theory 4
social model
  diversity 117
  see also under disability
social work, definition vii
South Africa 91
Standard Industrial Classification (SOC)
    78–80
stereotypes 4
structured dependency 48

Traveller Groups 94, 95–6
Turing, Alan 30

Union of the Physically Impaired Against
    Segregation (UPIAS) 57

Valuing people now: the delivery plan
    67–9

Whiteness 97–8
Williams, Fiona 59
Wolfenden Report 30–1
women *see* gender

Transforming Social Work Practice – titles in the series

Applied Psychology for Social Work (second edition)	ISBN 978 1 84445 356 6
Assessment in Social Work Practice	ISBN 978 1 84445 293 4
Collaborative Social Work Practice	ISBN 978 1 84445 014 5
Communication and Interpersonal Skills in Social Work (third edition)	ISBN 978 1 84445 610 9
Courtroom Skills for Social Workers	ISBN 978 1 84445 123 4
Critical Learning for Social Work Students	ISBN 978 1 84445 201 9
Effective Practice Learning in Social Work (second edition)	ISBN 978 1 84445 253 8
Equality and Diversity in Social Work Practice	ISBN 978 1 84445 593 5
Groupwork Practice in Social Work	ISBN 978 1 84445 086 2
Interprofessional Social Work: Effective Collaborative Approaches (second edition)	ISBN 978 1 84445 379 5
Introducing International Social Work	ISBN 978 1 84445 132 6
Loss and Social Work	ISBN 978 1 84445 088 6
Management and Organisations in Social Work (second edition)	ISBN 978 1 84445 216 3
Need, Risk and Protection in Social Work Practice	ISBN 978 1 84445 252 1
New Directions in Social Work Practice	ISBN 978 1 84445 079 4
Practical Computer Skills for Social Work	ISBN 978 1 84445 031 2
Proactive Child Protection and Social Work	ISBN 978 1 84445 131 9
Reflective Practice in Social Work (second edition)	ISBN 978 1 84445 364 1
Research Skills for Social Work	ISBN 978 1 84445 179 1
Safeguarding Adults in Social Work	ISBN 978 1 84445 148 7
Sensory Awareness and Social Work	ISBN 978 1 84445 293 4
Service User and Carer Participation in Social Work	ISBN 978 1 84445 074 9
Sexuality and Social Work	ISBN 978 1 84445 085 5
Social Policy and Social Work	ISBN 978 1 84445 301 6
Social Work and Human Development (third edition)	ISBN 978 1 84445 380 1
Social Work and Mental Health (third edition)	ISBN 978 1 84445 154 8
Social Work and Mental Health in Scotland	ISBN 978 1 84445 130 2
Social Work and Spirituality	ISBN 978 1 84445 194 4
Social Work in Education and Children's Services	ISBN 978 1 84445 045 9
Social Work Intervention	ISBN 978 1 84445 199 9

Social Work Practice: Assessment, Planning, Intervention and Review (third edition)	ISBN 978 1 84445 831 8
Social Work Skills with Adults	ISBN 978 1 84445 218 7
Social Work Skills with Children, Young People and their Families	ISBN 978 1 84445 346 7
Social Work with Children and Families (second edition)	ISBN 978 1 84445 144 9
Social Work with Children, Young People and their Families in Scotland (second edition)	ISBN 978 1 84445 156 2
Social Work with Drug and Substance Misusers (second edition)	ISBN 978 1 84445 262 0
Social Work with Looked After Children	ISBN 978 1 84445 103 6
Social Work with Older People (second edition)	ISBN 978 1 84445 155 5
Social Work with People with Learning Difficulties (second edition)	ISBN 978 1 84445 042 8
Sociology and Social Work	ISBN 978 1 84445 087 9
Studying for your Social Work Degree	ISBN 978 1 84445 174 6
Thriving and Surviving in Social Work	ISBN 978 1 84445 080 0
Understanding and Using Theory in Social Work	ISBN 978 1 84445 139 5
Using the Law in Social Work (fourth edition)	ISBN 978 1 84445 247 7
Values and Ethics in Social Work (second edition)	ISBN 978 1 84445 370 2
What is Social Work? Context and Perspectives (third edition)	ISBN 978 1 84445 248 4
Youth Justice and Social Work	ISBN 978 1 84445 066 4

To order, please contact our distributor: BEBC Distribution, Albion Close, Parkstone, Poole, BH12 3LL. Telephone: 0845 230 9000, email: **learningmatters@bebc.co.uk**. You can also find more information on each of these titles and our other learning resources at www.learningmatters.co.uk.